# THE COSMIC DETECTIVE

# THE
# COSMIC
# DETECTIVE

## EXPLORING THE MYSTERIES
## OF OUR UNIVERSE

DR MANI BHAUMIK

Introduction by Dr Edgar Mitchell,
Apollo 14 Astronaut

PUFFIN BOOKS

PUFFIN BOOKS
Published by the Penguin Group
Penguin Books India Pvt. Ltd, 11 Community Centre, Panchsheel Park, New Delhi 110 017, India
Penguin Group (USA) Inc., 375 Hudson Street, New York, New York 10014, USA
Penguin Group (Canada), 90 Eglinton Avenue East, Suite 700, Toronto, Ontario, M4P 2Y3, Canada (a division of Pearson Penguin Canada Inc.)
Penguin Books Ltd, 80 Strand, London WC2R 0RL, England
Penguin Ireland, 25 St Stephen's Green, Dublin 2, Ireland (a division of Penguin Books Ltd)
Penguin Group (Australia), 250 Camberwell Road, Camberwell, Victoria 3124, Australia (a division of Pearson Australia Group Pty Ltd)
Penguin Group (NZ), 67 Apollo Drive, Rosedale, North Shore 0632, New Zealand (a division of Pearson New Zealand Ltd)
Penguin Group (South Africa) (Pty) Ltd, 24 Sturdee Avenue, Rosebank, Johannesburg 2196, South Africa

Penguin Books Ltd, Registered Offices: 80 Strand, London WC2R 0RL, England

First published in Puffin by Penguin Books India 2008

Text copyright © Mani Bhaumik 2008
Pages 91–92 are an extension of the copyright page

All rights reserved

10 9 8 7 6 5 4 3 2 1

ISBN: 9780143330691

Typeset in Sabon MT by Eleven Arts, New Delhi

Printed at Gopsons Papers Ltd, Noida

*For*
*all the curious young minds*
*of the world*

*'The most beautiful experience we can have is the mysterious'*

—Albert Einstein

# Contents

# Acknowledgements

I wish to express my deep appreciation to all the scientists who have helped humankind with their tireless efforts to unravel the mysteries of our universe.

My special thanks go to A. W. Hill for his expert editorial help. My innate curiosity for the unknown found a match in his that led to many fruitful discussions. I am immensely grateful to astronaut Dr Edgar Mitchell for his inspiring introduction to the book as well as for providing his photograph taken on the surface of the moon. The skilful assistance of Tatiana Chekova in preparation of the manuscript is also greatly appreciated.

Finally, I would like to thank the National Aeronautics and Space Administration of USA, as well as the Space Telescope Science Institute and the Jet Propulsion Laboratory, for making available the beautiful, historic photographs used in this book.

Mani Bhaumik

# Introduction

O n a cloudy January afternoon in 1971, when we lifted off from Florida to land on the moon, we were too preoccupied during the entire trip with the overwhelming details of the mission to give much thought to the historic significance of our expedition. It did not dawn on me at the time that we were indeed vanguards, who were preparing humankind to be a spacefaring species.

Being the lunar module pilot, I could only get some respite from my duties following the lunar surface activities and after docking with Kitty Hawk, the craft that would take us back to Earth. Only then was I free to take it all in. I have expressed many times in books and lectures over the years the epiphany that was my experience of universal oneness, as I was looking at the distant oasis of Earth against the velvety darkness of space punctuated by stars and galaxies, normally only viewed through Earth-bound telescopes.

The intuitive leap that occurred presented me with the sort of mystery that the book, *The Cosmic Detective,* encourages you to pursue! A mystery that interweaves the very, very large with the very, very small and whose clues lay scattered over the entirety of time and space. A story bigger than any single individual, yet one which has you and me as its central characters. And I realized something else: no single person was going to solve it for me! Each of us must accept that mission.

Advances in science and technology, beginning in the late nineteenth century and continuing unabated throughout the twentieth century, have made it possible to envision and create a human role in the universe unimaginable to previous generations. Our adventure in space began by orbiting the Earth, moving on to exploring the moon, and was followed by teams of men and women learning to live and work in the International Space Station—the first outpost of a human community unhindered by national borders or tribal and religious conflicts.

These are magnificent first steps towards a destiny as citizens of the Universe. Another crowning achievement was the launching of the Hubble telescope into space. Hubble has provided stunningly clear pictures of distant galaxies and star systems, and may well lead to the discovery of habitable planets other than our own—planets suitable for the evolution of intelligent species. Without much doubt, I believe they are there.

Only in dreams and myths could our ancestors have glimpsed the majesty and beauty revealed to us by these leaps in science and technology. However, our technologies have also yielded enhanced tools for destruction and strife. It is up to us to direct our planetary civilization towards increased cooperation, harmony and peace rather than conflict and violence. Mani Bhaumik's book, written with young readers in mind, is a call to discover the potential and splendour that is possible if humankind heeds the call of the stars and makes the right choice.

July 2008                                Edgar Mitchell, Sc.D.,
                                            Apollo 14 astronaut,
                                           sixth man on the moon.

# The Starry Sky

The world is full of unsolved mysteries. In every community in every country, files are kept of cases the police have never been able to close, many dating from events that occurred long ago. Most of us like to think that with the right clues, we'd find the solution everyone else has missed.

Do you know what is the greatest unsolved mystery of all? It's the mystery of how our universe was made. None of us was there at that time. So how do we find out what happened? Fortunately, in this case, the evidence is all around us. We just need to know where and how to look. We have come a long way in tracking down this mystery. But the cosmic detectives are still far from closing the case with a verdict that is beyond reasonable doubt. Are you bold enough to try your luck?

Once upon a time I was your age, and like you, I was curious. You may live in the city, or the suburbs, or perhaps in a small rural hamlet. I was born in a tiny, primitive village far from the lights of any city. There was no electricity, and when night fell, only kerosene and oil lamps gave light. When those lamps went out, the darkness swallowed everything, and I spent night after night wishing to escape the poverty and hopelessness that hid within it. Yet, a different part of me—a bolder part—was thrilled when darkness fell over the village and the world fell silent. Let me tell you why.

I imagined there was a story spelled across the night skies with stars, a fairy tale more wondrous than any I had heard from my grandmother. It was the story of how even a poor boy like me could one day slay the dragons and enter the glittering palaces that hung like diamonds from the roof of heaven. If you have never seen the velvety darkness of a night sky, it may be hard for you to picture how spectacular the stars can be, or how mysterious it is that they seem close enough to touch and yet more distant than anything we can imagine.

Almost every night I lost myself in this mystery, and the further out into the stars my thoughts took me, the more mysterious they became. While I was still quite young, I decided that if ever I were to devote my life fully to a single goal, it would be to unravel the mystery of the starry sky. And it wouldn't be only to conquer dragons or capture castles. I believed the stars offer something else, something even more magical: the answer to where we come from and what we are made of.

At that time, few great scientists were studying these things with much seriousness. The science of cosmology—the study of our universe and how it came into being—was still in its infancy. You, the young explorers of today, are the lucky ones. The study of the cosmos and its vast, uncharted regions is now going on at full speed throughout the world. And we are discovering things that are stranger than our wildest dreams.

As a boy, I used to wonder how many stars were there. I even tried to count them, and ran out of numbers. Where had they come from, these uncountable, brilliant stars that appeared each night against the black canvas of the sky? Would they shine forever, or did they live and die as people do? How far away were they? Were there other worlds like ours out there, with other boys and girls like me asking the same questions? Did the universe have a birthday, and if so, who helped it to celebrate? Did we have to go to the stars for the answers, or were there people who knew?

What I didn't realize, as a lonely boy in a remote village, was that I was asking the same questions that people—old and young, rich and poor, wise and simple—had been asking for thousands of years. And like my most distant ancestors, I believed that the stars I could see on the clearest nights were all the stars that existed. I couldn't have known then that the stars were all around me, like a field of fireflies on a summer night, and that I was part of this field. I couldn't have known that I was indeed made of stardust!

When I grew up and came to the city for my education, the night sky was filled with other lights, and the stars shone less brightly. People who live in the city can almost forget that stars exist. But I carried with me my memories of those dark nights in a village without electricity, a place where people sleep and rise with the sun. These memories were like a seed planted in my mind, a seed that would grow into a lifelong aspiration to solve the mystery written long, long ago in those starry skies.

With the eyes of a mature scientist, I have searched since then for clues, and I am happy to say that from the efforts of other scientists and seekers, I have been able to gather many of them—enough to get you started on your own investigation. Over the last hundred years, and especially in the past fifty, our picture of the universe has become much clearer. We now have a very good idea of how old the most distant stars are, and how they were made. We even have a reliable indication of how big the universe is, and believe me, it is bigger than anything you can think of. But with each clue that is discovered, another mystery appears; so there will be plenty of them for you to solve.

When I was your age, I imagined that if I could build a home in the middle of the stars, I would come closer to understanding their secrets. I thought that if I could look into the heart of their light, I could read their story. I was not far from the truth, because as we shall see, the light from the stars holds many of the clues to their beginnings. Today, my childhood dream has come very close to being fulfilled, although not in quite the way I pictured it. We may not be able to travel to the stars any time soon, because even the nearest of them—a star called Proxima Centauri—would take the fastest spaceship we can now build many human lifetimes to reach. But that won't keep us from making the stars our next-door neighbours.

Imagine that you could sit in your bedroom and send your eyes any place in the world—any place in the universe, for that matter. Seeing a place may not be quite as nice as being there, but if we can see it well enough—the way we see a movie or a video game, for example—we can get a pretty good idea of what it would be like to be there. In just a few decades' time, we have launched a number of marvellous 'eyes in the skies' into our nearby space. The best known of them are the Hubble Space Telescope (pic. 1) and the International Space Station (pic. 4), but equally revealing are the COBE (Cosmic Background Explorer) satellite (pic. 3), launched in 1989, and its successor, the WMAP (Wilkinson Microwave Anisotropy Probe).

We will learn more in the coming chapters about what these roaming eyes have shown us about the cosmos, but the important thing to know now is that once we travel outside

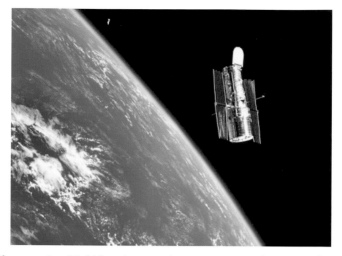

1. The amazing Hubble telescope in space. It is as large as a bus and moving with a velocity of 17,000 miles per hour, in an orbit 400 miles above Earth. Still, it can keep its focus trained on a dime from 200 miles afar. Many historic discoveries in space have been made possible with this unique telescope. It can show us how the universe was like 13 billion years ago. Using this telescope, scientists estimate that there are at least 125 billion galaxies in the universe.

2. An unmanned probe on the surface of Mars. Other space probes have been sent to all the planets of the solar system. With the help of numerous pictures sent by these space probes, we have been able to know many of the mysteries of our solar family. We have seen that most of the planets and their satellites consist of solid real estate like our Earth.

3. With the help of this COBE satellite, we have been able to gather the most significant fingerprints to unravel the cosmic detective story. It has helped us to close in on the moment of birth of the universe. The Nobel Prize in physics in 2006 was awarded for the discoveries made possible by COBE.

4. As large as two football fields and weighing 1 million pounds is this International Space Station. It is visible in the night sky as a slowly moving point of light. In addition to many international working astronauts, so far four space tourists have visited this station. Several plans are on the drawing board for a space hotel for tourists to go on vacation. The space station can help us for preparations needed to go to another planet.

5. This is an example of a spiral galaxy in the shape of a dish. About 200 billion stars reside in such a galaxy. The stars are revolving in orderly circular orbits around the centre of this galaxy.

6. Another example of a spiral galaxy. Huge amounts of gas and dust clouds inside the spiral arms are giving rise to many new stars. This is why the spiral galaxies look the brightest in space. These galaxies resemble in their appearance the hurricanes on Earth.

7. Photograph of a hurricane over the Caribbean taken from space.

*The Sun*

8. You can see the approximate location of our solar family in another spiral galaxy similar to ours. The centre of the galaxy is a very dangerous place. Being in the outskirts of the galaxy, we can live safely from the hectic activities at the centre.

9. A photograph of our own Milky Way galaxy taken by infrared light. As you can see, the side view of the galaxy is like a dish. At the central bulge there are numerous older stars and quite possibly a black hole.

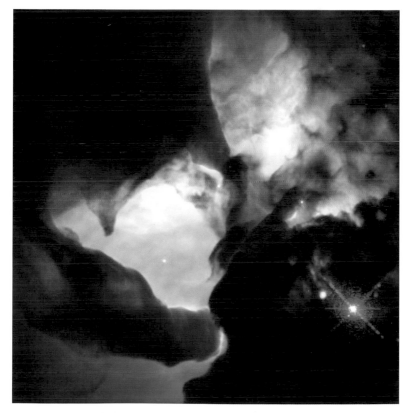

10. Very vast is this Lagoon nebula. Many new stars are being born in its gas and dust cloud. We are all made of such stardust.

11. A dramatic portion of the Orion nebula, where about 3,000 stars of different sizes are being born in the gas and dust cloud.

12. A stellar nursery in Eagle nebula.

13. Many stars and planets are being born in this part of the Swan nebula.

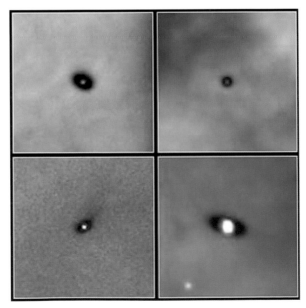

14. Four protostars are taking shape with a protoplanetary disc around each of them. The discs look dark since they are silhouette images against the background light of the nebula. It may sound surprising that without the simultaneous formation of planets and their moons, most of the stars could not be born. This is why the number of planets and their satellites in the universe are innumerable.

the earth's hazy atmosphere into space, we are suddenly able to see very clearly for very, very long distances. And when we see a long way into space, we also see something else. It is something that may sound more like science fiction than science, but it is absolutely true and absolutely essential to the detective work you are about to undertake.

What is the most valuable tool that a detective could have? A tool so powerful that no clue could be hidden from him? It would be the ability to see back in time to the moment when the event he or she is investigating occurred. An ordinary detective must attempt this through the careful assembling of evidence, but he can't actually see the past as it happened. You, the cosmic detective, can, because, in a sense, the universe is a time machine.

When we observe an object, what we are actually observing is the light which travels from the object to our eyes. If the light of the stars had never been turned on, we would not know they were there at all. Light travels through space at a speed which is the same everywhere in the universe. This speed is 186,282.4 miles or 299,792.5 kilometres per second. That's fast—faster than anything else in nature— but it's not instantaneous. Because the universe is so enormous and the distances between stars so great, it takes time for their light to reach us, and that means when we look out at distant objects in space, we are also looking back in time. We see them not as they are, *but as they were* when their light began its journey to us.

For example, it takes approximately 1.3 seconds for the light of the moon to make its way to earth, which means that when we look up at the moon, we see it as it was 1.3 seconds ago. The sun's light takes nearly 8.34 minutes to reach us, so we see the sun 8.34 minutes ago. Things get very strange, however, when we consider objects that are much further away. The light we observe today from the little star cluster known as the Pleiades (the Seven Sisters) left 440 years ago, so we see the Pleiades as they were in the mid sixteenth century. And if you want to feel a chill up your spine, consider the possibility that when we train our telescopes on truly distant stars, we may be seeing light from objects which no longer even exist. When stars die, they are survived by their light, which streams across the cold, empty vastness like a ghost haunting the countless mansions in space.

All of this means, of course, that the further we look out into space, the further we look back in time, and that if we could see to the very edge of the universe, we would be seeing the beginning of time. What—you ask—time has a beginning? Well, yes, at least in our universe, which is the only one we know of so far. Evidence gathered by the WMAP satellite and other studies prove beyond much doubt that the universe is 13.7 billion years old, give or take a hundred million. How big is it? At least as big as the distance that light can travel in 13.7 billion years, and when you consider how fast light moves, that is a distance beyond comprehension. Where did the universe come from and how did it come into being? This is a job for the cosmic detective.

The investigation can begin with 'getting to know' our own corner of the cosmos. However, detectives must take in the bigger picture before they can focus on the details. As we travel deeper into space, we will gradually uncover many secrets of the universe, for like the oceans of the earth once explored by sailors like Magellan and Columbus, the cosmos shares its treasures only with those bold enough to seek them.

With each question we answer, though, another will arise. As the great astrophysicist Sir Arthur Eddington said, 'The universe is not only stranger than we imagine, it is stranger than we *can* imagine.' For example, the WMAP satellite and other studies mentioned earlier determined that the universe is made of *only* 4 per cent ordinary matter (the stuff we can see, touch and measure), and 96 per cent dark matter and dark energy. What are dark matter and dark energy? No one knows yet, and we can't see or touch them, but as we'll learn, the universe—as we know it—wouldn't exist without them.

After we have surveyed the outlying territory, we'll return to our own immediate neighbourhood and do a little serious field work. The best clues are often found close to home. Then, finally, we will explore some of the wilder regions of the universe and some of the wilder ideas about it, so that we can begin to put together our own conjecture of the case.

A classic detective story asks not only who, where, and how, but *why*. And the why of the universe is the most puzzling question of all. You may find as you investigate that things get cloudier before they get clearer, and sometimes even a little bit daunting. But if you decide to accept this case, rest assured that I will stay with you, and provide as much assistance as I can, as did Dr Watson to Sherlock Holmes.

There is much evidence to be gathered before we have the full picture. Lucky for us, nature has left much of the evidence 'hidden in plain sight' throughout the cosmos. The trail of this evidence leads us grippingly close to the very beginning, when science tells us that all that we see in the starry sky and all that lies beyond it came from a seed tantalizingly far, far smaller than the full stop at the end of this sentence.

To get you started with your investigation, let me give you a bit of encouragement. As strange, immense and complex as the universe may seem, you are as important a part of it as any other. That's right. Some of the most notable cosmologists are now saying that, in effect, the universe is not complete without each and every one of us. What exactly does this mean? And what does it mean when some of those same scientists tell us that the observer of the universe cannot be separated from what he or she observes? These questions are as much a part of our case as how the universe was made.

We'll have to proceed step by step and fingerprint by fingerprint, sorting and sifting and compiling the evidence until it makes for a convincing account. And like all good detectives, we'll begin with what is right in front of our eyes.

# Our Home in the Stars

O n very clear, dark nights, if you are far away from the lights of the city, something spectacular appears in the sky. Once you have seen it, you can never forget it, and you may be on your way to a career as a cosmic detective. Once your eyes get used to the dark, you see dozens, then hundreds, of twinkling stars. Suddenly, as if by the stroke of a magic wand, there is an enormous, glowing river of white light sweeping across the roof of the sky—a river made of billions and billions of stars. Only after you catch your breath do you say to yourself, 'Ah, this must be the Milky Way.'

When we see the Milky Way galaxy for the first time, almost all of us think it is something 'out there' in space, probably far away from where we live. Well, it is and it isn't. Truly, most of the stars we see in that luminous river are very, very distant, and the Milky Way is 100,000 light years across. A reminder: a light year is the distance that light can travel in one year, and that distance is approximately 5.9 trillion miles or 9.46 trillion kilometres! But the Milky Way is also our home in the universe; so when we look out towards its brilliant, busy centre, it is as if we are looking at the lights of the city from a quiet suburb on its outskirts. We live inside the Milky Way. We are part of it.

More precisely, we live about two-thirds of the way out from our galaxy's central hub, on a small planet orbiting one of its 200 billion or more stars. So, in a way, each and every one of us grows up in a small, isolated village, far, far away from the blazing heart of the city.

Galaxies are the largest structures in the universe—unless we count galactic clusters and super clusters—and their primary activity is to make stars. (A galaxy is essentially home to a huge assembly of stars, gas and dust as well as some other exotic matter, all held together by their mutual gravitational attraction). We now know that there may be more galaxies in the universe than there are individual stars in any one galaxy—the current count is at least 125 billion of them—and that's based only on what we have been able to identify so far with the latest technology. They come in three basic shapes and sizes—spiral, elliptical, and irregular—but all of them are star-making factories. Before we head out to take a tour of our galaxy, it may be a good time to say a few words about what a star is and how the galaxies make them.

Like most children, my first impression of the stars was that they were tiny lights, as in the nursery rhyme, 'Twinkle, twinkle, little star.' When I grew up I came to know that those twinkling lights are actually enormous balls of fire, much hotter than the hottest oven. Our star is the sun, but because it is 93,000,000 miles away, it warms rather than burns us (except when we stay out in it too long!). Most bright stars are at least as big as our sun, which is a fairly typical bright star in the middle of its life. They appear little only because they are so far away—think of how small, for example, airplanes look from the ground. To get an idea of just how large an ordinary star is, imagine how big a sphere earth is, and then consider that the sun is roughly a million times that big. Have you ever tried to count to a million?

You might think of stars as solid objects, like the earth, but this is not really the case. Our star, the sun, began its life about 4.6 billion years ago as a huge, swirling cloud of gas and dust, made mostly of the element of hydrogen. As the cloud swirled, eventually it began to condense and collapse under the force of its own gravity, and due to the pressure, the temperature at its core rose gradually. (A 'law of nature': as things get squeezed together, they get hotter!) It spun faster and faster, flattening into a whirling disc, its centre getting hotter and hotter. Finally, the heat at the central core ignited the fires of atomic fusion, converting hydrogen into helium and radiating light energy in all directions. A star was born— as a gigantic ball of very hot dense gas, not a solid.

Our galaxy has produced at least two hundred billion stars this way, and it is still making them. As we shall see, it has also made planets like our earth.

If we were to travel outside the Milky Way and look back at it from deep space, we would see that it resembles a bigger (much bigger!) version of the swirling star cloud described above: an enormous rotating stellar disc a hundred thousand light years across, and roughly a thousand light years thick, with spiral arms and a huge, bright bulge at the centre. In cosmic terms, that means it's as flat as a dish and shaped like a rotating pinwheel. How do we know it rotates? Because, astronomers have detected that every star in the galaxies like Milky Way orbits the galactic centre.

In fact, the Milky Way is a typical spiral galaxy, and spiral galaxies appear to be the busiest and brightest galaxies in the universe. The spiral is one of the basic shapes in nature. Look at a photograph (pic. 7) in this book of a hurricane over the Caribbean and compare it to the photographs (pics. 5, 6, 8) of the galaxies. Do you see the amazing similarity between the spiral arms of the galaxy and the spiral arms of the hurricane? Could there be some common element in the formation of these spirals, even though their origin and purpose are very different? The answer is probably yes, although the centre of a hurricane is almost empty while the core bulge of a galaxy is densely packed with stars. But in each case, there exists a central force pulling on everything around them. Now here is a question for the cosmic detective to ponder: a hurricane forms in our atmosphere, but how can there be rotating spirals in seemingly 'empty' space and what could stabilize their orderly rotations? A hint— there is a kind of exotic matter that we cannot see: dark matter, and there is more of it in the universe than the stuff we can see!

It is in the spiral arms of our galaxy that new stars are made, and it is right on the inside edge of one of these arms— known as the Orion Arm—that our sun and solar system reside. This is our home in the stars. Other arms have names like Perseus, Sagittarius, and even Norma!

How do we know what our galaxy looks like, or how big it is, if we are living inside it? After all, could someone living deep within a huge city tell you what the city looked like from the outside? The answer begins with telescopes and ends with some very advanced technology.

Since the early days of astronomy, the power of telescopes has increased almost beyond imagination. If you were to go to the moon and strike a match, there are telescopes on earth today that are powerful enough to see the flare. And now that we have launched super-telescopes like the Hubble and the Chandra X-Ray Observatory into space, we can see far, far beyond our galaxy and billions of years back in time. No matter how powerful our telescopes are, we still can't see the far side of the Milky Way from where we live. So we determine its shape by observing other galaxies that seem to behave in the same way.

The nearest galaxy, Andromeda (pic. 29), can actually be seen with the naked eye as a tiny fuzzy ball of light in the night sky. It was from the behaviour of certain types of stars in the Andromeda galaxy, an astronomer discovered that our Milky Way was not the only island of light in the cosmos, and after that the list of discoveries kept on growing. In this book you can see photographs of several magnificent spiral galaxies that look so similar to the Milky Way. The relative location of our sun has also been indicated in one of these galaxies.

Of the estimated 200 billion or more stars in the Milky Way, we can only see about 5,000 with our bare eyes. Why so few? Because, remember that our galaxy is shaped almost like a dish; and being inside the dish, we can only see the stars nearest to us. The rest are hidden by the diffuse interstellar gas and dust, some of which exist as enormous clouds that are known as nebulae. (Nebulae is plural for nebula, which means cloud in Latin. A nebula can be an aggregate of gas and dust from a single dying star as well as a subsequent vast collection of them.)

However, when our telescopes are adapted to look at the galaxy through infrared light, they penetrate the dust and gas, and we can see from our place in the 'suburbs' that the Milky Way appears like a dish—or a flying saucer—seen from the edge on. Look at the picture (pic. 9) taken by the COBE satellite using infrared light. You can also see that in the central bulge, the stars are closely packed together, becoming more sparse as we move to the outskirts. These central stars are older and more yellow than the young, blue stars found in the arms. But there are even older stars in the spherical halo that surrounds our galactic dish in space, some of them as old as the Milky Way itself. These great-grandfather stars are gathered in beehives of light known as globular clusters, orbiting to the very farthest reaches of the galactic halo.

Other spiral galaxies look and behave pretty much as ours does and that suggests a remarkable consistency in the universe. Why do you suppose, in a place so immense, there is such uniformity of design?

When I say immense, it is no exaggeration. If each spiral galaxy contains 100 to 400 billion stars, and scientists now estimate that there are at least 125 billion galaxies in the part of the universe that we can see, how many stars are there in the sky? How can we even comprehend such a number?

But there is an even more mind-boggling and magical thing about the universe than its size, age, and miraculously consistent design and mechanics, and it relates directly to you and me and that fairy tale I read as a boy in words written in the stars. As we continue our investigation of the cosmos, uncovering clue after clue about its origin, we will begin to see that we are made of 'fairy dust' spun out by the stars. Stardust. In the truest sense, we are all princes and princesses because we are the sons and daughters of the stars. But what is stardust? Notice the photograph of the vast Lagoon nebula (pic. 10).

Nebulae, among the most beautiful and awe-inspiring forms in the universe, are found woven throughout the spiral arms of our galaxy. They are the most active star-making regions. These nebulae (pics. 10, 11, 12, 13, 23) are giant clouds of gas and dust which gather from the material blown out by dying stars. You see, the universe wastes nothing—stars die and many more are born from it. Nebulae contain the raw ingredients of both the stars and of us.

The primordial atomic elements of the universe were hydrogen and helium. These light elements are able to make a star, but not us. For life like ours to be possible, additional heavier elements such as carbon, oxygen and nitrogen are required. These elements were forged inside the nuclear furnaces of the first generation of stars, where the temperature was sufficient to cause smaller elements to fuse into larger ones. When these first generation stars died, they dispersed most of their mass into space. The dust and gas of these exploded stars assembled to form the nebulae.

Nebulae are made of stardust, and so are we. If we study the birth of a star like our sun, we will understand a little better how and why this is so.

Let's imagine we are in a time machine and return to that time, 4.6 billion years ago, to have a closer look at when our sun was coming into being. We see a disorganized swirl of gas and dust about 15 trillion miles across. Then suddenly a disturbance, perhaps caused by the explosion of a nearby star, sends ripples through the cloud, stirring the gas and dust particles, nudging them closer and closer. Eventually, sufficient gravitational attraction occurs, when they begin to clump together and interact. This interaction causes them to spin increasingly faster, and as the dense cloud spins, it flattens into a disc. In about 10 million years, the material at the centre of the disc becomes a protostar that will ultimately become our sun. Within about 20 million years, the disc around the protostar becomes a protoplanetary disc or proplyd. In the photograph (pic. 14) you can see four protostars being formed, each having a protoplanetary disc associated with it. The discs look dark since they are silhouette images of the proplyds against the background light of the nebula.

Our earth began as planetesimals formed from the grains of dust in the whirlwind of the protoplanetary disc, and in time coalesced to form the planet, gathering all the elements required to fashion the complex and varied ecosystem necessary for life. It all began with stardust.

If it happened here, in our little neighbourhood of the universe, could earth-like planets have formed in other neighbourhoods as well? We have yet to visit another planet or get a close-up view of other solar systems, but you will be surprised to know that science gives us strong reasons to believe that *the formation of planets is the rule rather than an exception in the universe.* The Hubble telescope observation of a protoplanetary disc around each of the protostars directly confirms this rule for the first time. Except for a small percentage of what are called binary star systems—where two stars are born together like twins and spend their lives going around one another—most stars come into being along with their planetary systems for conservation of angular momentum, which is a measure of the consistency of angular motion (another one of the many 'laws of nature' that makes the earth rotate once every twenty-four hours). Only about 1 per cent of the angular motion of our solar system resides in the sun; the rest is borne by the planets, all orbiting in the same direction as the rotation of the sun and in a plane along the sun's equator. This is credible evidence that except for the binaries, a star cannot form unless the planets pick up most of the angular motion of the whirling dust cloud. Nearly half the sun-like stars in a spiral galaxy are expected to be orbited by planets. There are also other, more numerous stars smaller than the sun, called red dwarfs, all of which are believed to have planetary systems.

The planets do not burn nuclear fuel and have no light of their own. They shine only by the reflected light of their suns. That is why we can observe the planets in our solar system only against the darkness of the night sky. Farther away, the light reflected by planets of other solar systems is so faint compared to the light radiated by their suns that we cannot see them with today's telescopes.

Evidence of their presence has been observed, however, by the gravitational 'wobble' in the motion of their stars, and scientists are quite confident about their existence. What do I mean by gravitational 'wobble'? When a planet orbits a star, each exerts gravitational attraction on the other. The force exerted upon the star by the planet causes it to move around in a miniature orbit in space, which is a tiny copy of the planet's orbit. This wobble of a star can tell us when a planet is in the neighbourhood exerting its force on the star, even though we cannot see the planet directly.

Assuming stars like our sun to have, on an average, six planets in their systems, can you now calculate how many planets there are in just the 125 billion galaxies we know are out there, each containing about 100 billion stars?

If you have begun to think like a detective, you may also be wondering about something even more important. If there are innumerable planetary systems like ours in this universe, is it possible that intelligent life exists *only* on Earth? Now there is another great mystery worth pursuing!

Here is your first investigative assignment. We have learned that stars in our galaxy are formed in rotating discs of gas and dust, and that all stars, in turn, rotate around the centre of the galaxy, causing it to spin in space like a giant pinwheel. What makes the Milky Way spin? Using the Internet, the library, and your own detective's intuition, see if you can make a guess about why so many things in the universe seem to be in rotation. Take another glimpse of the picture of a hurricane. Think about other spirals in nature and how they are formed. Is there a connection?

# To Live and Die as a Star

Long before even your great-grandfather was born, in the year 1837, astronomers with their telescopes trained on the southern skies noticed that a tiny pinpoint of light known as Eta Carinae had suddenly started to get brighter, and wondered what could account for it. We now know that this pinpoint is actually one of the most massive stars in our galaxy, 8,000 light years away and about 5 million times as bright as our sun. And we know something else. The reason Eta Carinae got brighter is that it was beginning to die. Have you ever noticed the way a candle burns brighter before it goes out?

We have seen a glimpse of how stars are born. Now we must also look at how they die. Like all things in nature, stars do not live forever. Even our sun will die one day, but there is no reason to panic. It won't happen for about 5 billion years, and by then, human beings may have moved to an entirely different part of the universe! The death of a star may seem like a sad thing, but as we have seen in the previous chapter, the birth of new stars are made possible by the death of old ones.

Did you also get the hint of something else very significant? Did you notice that gravity—which operates on a large scale—and fusion—which operates on a small scale—

act in concert to stabilize the star? Could this relationship of the very large and the very small be an important clue in our detective mystery? Possibly. Let us examine some more evidence by investigating further details of the birth and death of stars (pic. 15).

Close your eyes and try to imagine flying into the centre of a colossal luminous cloud of gas and stardust like the famous Eagle Nebula, piled as much as 400 trillion miles high and 300 trillion miles wide, made from the material hurled into space by stars that have blown apart. As we soar through regions of brilliant blue, red and green, ducking and diving like Luke Skywalker, the character from *Star Wars*, we see the cloud is clearing in certain places, revealing ten, twenty, fifty new stars born at the same time and glittering like diamonds. In other places, there are dark patches of cooler, denser gas and dust which are in the earlier stages of star formation.

As gravity pulls the raw material in on itself, large balls form in the centre of each cloud, like pearls in an oyster. These are the protostars. They are covered with a dense cloud of gas that is ultimately blown away by the heat produced by the contracting protostar. At the core of a ball, the temperature rises gradually as the collisions of dust and gas increase and intensify with continuing contraction. Eventually when the temperature at the core reaches 10 million degrees Centigrade, nuclear fusion of hydrogen into helium begins. With fusion comes energy released in the form of brilliant light, and from a safe distance we witness and say, 'Ahhh. What a beautiful star!'

Stars are not born alike, any more than babies are. Some are born big and others quite small. There are runt stars born about one tenth the size (radius) of our sun, and giants one hundred times bigger. The size of the star depends upon the amount of gas and dust gathered during its formation. The brightest superstar can be almost 150 times as bulky as the sun. The smallest star observed is just about ten times less massive than our sun, but having a size only as small as that of the planet Jupiter. The smaller stars are quite dim, but they live much longer. These are the red dwarf stars we encountered earlier, which are more abundant in the universe.

The colours of the stars also differ. Some are bluish (hottest), some are reddish (coolest), and some—like our sun—are yellowish (that is, somewhere in between). The surface temperature of the hottest stars can be over 40,000 degrees, while the coolest stars are as low as 2,500 degrees. Our sun's surface temperature is about 6,000 degrees.

The time it takes for a protostar to become a star depends upon its mass as well. Our sun took a total of about 30 million years to become a star. Heavier stars contract faster and are born quicker. A star fifteen times the mass of the sun takes only about 160,000 years, while a star five times less massive than the sun can take a billion years to be born.

Life is a constant struggle even for the stars (just ask any movie star!). Being a star is a balancing act between contraction and expansion. On one hand, the force of gravity—the same force which keeps the planets in their orbits and our feet on the ground—is attracting every part of the star to the centre, while the huge amount of energy produced by the nuclear fusion at the centre is pushing everything outwards. A stable star, also called a main sequence star, is formed when the two forces are in balance. This balance is maintained as long as there is sufficient hydrogen fuel in the star. When all the hydrogen has been converted to helium, the star begins to die and gravity gains the upper hand. In the end, gravity wins this fight, and the star collapses in one way or another. But the excitement isn't over yet.

The attraction of gravity starts to win when the star's nuclear fuel begins to diminish, as it does eventually in all stars. When this happens, gravity causes the star to begin contracting—to fall in on itself in a kind of replay of the process that occurred during its birth. As a result of this contraction, the new energy produced at the centre gives the star a sort of 'second wind', like a runner who gets a burst of strength a few metres from the finish line. Before the death of a star like our sun, it puts up a last battle against the inward attraction of gravity by nuclear fusion of helium into carbon. In more massive stars, even heavier elements are formed in stages.

During this dramatic phase, nuclear fusion also begins to occur in whatever hydrogen is left in the shell surrounding the core. The outer tiers of the shell expand from the heat of fusion, making the star bigger. The core contracts further as its fusion fuel is gradually depleted. The contraction releases radiation energy causing the envelope to expand even more, making the star much bigger than it ever was—as much as a hundred or more times bigger, increasing its brightness to observers like us. The temperature decreases in the expanding envelope, shifting the colour from yellow to bright red and, fittingly, it is known as a red giant. Every fairy tale needs a giant, right? You can see a picture (pic. 16) of how big a red giant of the sky can be.

There are two ways in which the life story of a star can end: violently, with an explosion that is the biggest fireworks show in the universe, or gently, with hardly a hint to let you know it was once a great source of light. Our sun will go calmly, as do all stars its size or smaller. Let's look at both endings.

## THE DEATH OF A SMALLER STAR: WHITE DWARF

A star the size of our sun will eventually become a red giant, and finally give its outer shells back to the universe in the form of a planetary nebula, so that new stars and solar systems can be made. As the envelope is cast off, the core of the huge star becomes as small as the earth. We call such a star a white dwarf.

The core of a white dwarf is so dense that one teaspoonful of it on earth could weigh about five tons—as much as a truck. Inside a white dwarf, the tightly compressed electrons produce a quantum repulsive force that balances the inward gravitational attraction, and the star again achieves a sort of stability, even though all its fuel has burned out. It radiates its remaining trapped energy into the planetary nebula, which creates a beautiful glow. You can see in the photographs (pics. 17, 18, 19, 20) taken by the Hubble Space Telescope what a wonderful sight that is!

A white dwarf loses its light and heat over billions of years and eventually becomes a cold black mass. That's when we call it a black dwarf. This—a long, long time from now—will be the fate of our sun.

## THE DEATH OF A LARGE STAR: SUPERNOVA

A star having a mass of at least eight times that of our sun meets a different fate. It might make sense to think that big stars, with all their mass and fuel, live longer than small stars, but just the opposite is true. Big stars are also hungrier and go through their fuel much faster. While this takes billions of years with a star like our sun, it can happen in only millions with truly massive stars. Once all the hydrogen at the star's core has fused to become helium, it starts to become a red supergiant, a helium core surrounded by an expanding shell of gas. Over the next million years, its core shrinks as nuclear reactions progressively create other heavier elements in a structure resembling onion shells, eventually forming a centre made of iron where the core temperature rises to 5 billion degrees or more.

Iron cannot burn to create the energy of nuclear fusion, and the inward attraction of the star's gravity is first balanced by quantum repulsion of electrons as in the white dwarfs. But the strong gravitational force of the massive star overpowers the electrons, squeezing them into the nucleus to form neutrons. With the loss of electrons, there is nothing to oppose the inward pressure. As a result, gravity rapidly crushes the core from about the size of the earth to a sphere of only ten to twenty kilometres in diameter, when quantum repulsion of neutrons resists further compression. This core collapse occurres in less than the time it takes you to snap your fingers, triggering a reverse shock wave within the collapsing shells and then an explosion of such mind-boggling magnitude that even from tens of thousands of light years away, it becomes visible as the brightest object in the night sky. In fact, the energy released during core collapse can be many times larger than the energy produced by our sun during its entire life of 10 billion years. We call such an exploding star a supernova, and there is hardly anything like it in the universe. Supernovae figure in many myths and legends of the past, including the story of the three wise men who are believed by some to have followed a bright star to the birthplace of Jesus of Nazareth.

Supernovae are vital events in the development of our universe. The shock waves that travel from the core of the collapsed star at speeds of as much as 30,000 miles per second pass through the shells of gas surrounding the core, generating pressures and temperatures necessary for fostering the creation of all the elements heavier than iron. The ensuing outward rushing shells are explosive enough to blast themselves into space at speeds up to 10,000 miles per second. These layers consist of elements which include carbon, oxygen, nitrogen, and silicon, the building blocks of worlds like ours, and of life as well.

The resulting nebula consists of about 95 per cent of the destroyed star, its colossal brilliance rising to a maximum and then fading, all within just a few months. The elements thrown into space (pic. 24) by the blast gather with those of other expired stars to form giant molecular gas clouds like the Eagle Nebula. As we have seen, these clouds are the nurseries where new solar systems are born, many holding the possibility for the development of life. Now you see again why we are all made of stardust.

The supernova explosions also control the evolution of galaxies. It is very likely that the birth of our solar system was initiated by the disturbance created when the shock wave from a nearby supernova passed through the lanes of gas and dust in a spiral arm of our galaxy. We probably owe our lives to an exploding star! It can truly be said that supernova explosions seed the universe with the potential for complex forms of matter like mountains, trees and people.

Before we extend our investigation even deeper into the cosmos—and ask you to do further detective work—I want to introduce some more mysterious objects connected with the death of stars. These cosmic mysteries are known as neutron stars, black holes and quasars.

## Neutron Stars

A star eight to twenty-five times bigger than our sun dies as a supernova with its iron core so compacted by gravity that all its atoms are crushed into one super dense mass of neutrons. At this point it becomes what is known as a neutron star. It is the densest object in the universe; in fact, so dense that a single teaspoonful on earth would weigh millions of tons. The neutron stars measuring only about ten kilometres rotate like spinning tops at an unbelievably fast rate—observed to be as much as 716 times a second. The rotational speed at the periphery approaches 10 per cent of the speed of light. It should be expected that something spinning that rapidly might create some strange effects, and it does indeed.

Due to their intense magnetic fields, the rotating neutron stars (pic. 25) radiate a narrow beam of electromagnetic radiation, much of which falls within the range we identify as radio waves. As a star like this rotates, the directed beam of radiation, which is not usually aligned with its axis of rotation, sweeps through space like a lighthouse beacon. If the earth happens to be in the path of the sweeping beam, a regular, pulsed radio signal is detected as if coming from a transmitter in space. The neutron stars whose rotating beam can be observed from earth are called pulsars.

In 1967, when signals from a pulsar were first picked up in the UK, scientists believed for a while that they might actually be radio communications from an alien civilization! The news was so startling that it remained a state secret for a few weeks. The scientists named their discovery

LGM-1, for 'Little Green Men'. Yes, even scientists have a sense of humour!

## BLACK HOLES

In the ancient mythology of Greece, the Minotaur is a monster with the head of a bull and body of a man that lives in the centre of a great spiral maze known as the Labyrinth and devours anyone foolish (or lost) enough to come near. At the centre of our galaxy—and quite possibly at the centre of all spiral galaxies—there also live monsters that swallow anything and everything in their reach. These monsters are known as black holes, which may conceal some of the clues to the greatest unsolved mysteries of the universe. Are you brave enough to take a look inside?

A black hole is created when a star at least twenty-five times larger (and often much more) than our sun dies. The development proceeds like the making of a neutron star and the resultant supernova. But because the initial mass of the star is so much greater, the forces pulling its core inward are also much stronger, so much so that it overwhelms the repulsive force of neutrons, and the entire mass of the star's core is squeezed instantly into a space smaller than the head of a pin—actually much smaller than the nucleus of a single atom.

Stop for a moment and try to visualize this. Start with the furniture in your room, then your house, then your city, then the sun and all its planets, and then twenty-five suns and all their planets, and then cram all of it into a place so tiny that not even the most powerful microscope can find it.

How dense would such an object be? How much gravitational force would it exert? So much that not even light could escape it. That's why we call them black holes.

Nothing in the universe can travel faster than the speed of light, and since light can't come out of the black hole, nothing else can either (well, nothing except possibly for some very weak radiation known as Hawking radiation).

Black holes trap light, yet, strangely enough, the area around a black hole—such as the one at the centre of our galaxy—is very bright. That's because a black hole is like a cosmic sinkhole, sucking all the surrounding material into its centre. As stars and planets and any other matter that happens to be in the neighbourhood are drawn into the vortex, they begin to spin around it, forming what is called an accretion disc. The disc becomes extremely hot and starts to radiate light, allowing us to observe the material inside (pic. 26) before it is swallowed up. Analysing the motion of the material in the accretion disc using the light emanating from it, scientists can determine the mass of the black hole.

There are two types of black holes. The mass of an ordinary black hole is the remains of a star about twenty-five to a hundred times more massive than our sun. Another type of black hole can become so large with accretion of matter, especially during the early stages of galaxy formation, that its mass can equal that of 10 billion suns.

## QUASARS

The giant black holes are believed to power what are known as quasars, among the oldest and most distant objects in the universe. The light of a quasar comes from the compact accretion region of the massive black hole. So much light is radiated by quasars (they can be a trillion times as bright as our sun) that we can see them like a point-like star (pic. 27) from 10 billion light years away. The black hole at the centre of our galaxy is not as big as these ancient monsters, but it is big enough to be called super massive. It is called by the name Sagittarius A*, and it has a mass roughly 3.7 million times that of the sun. Could there be a beast chasing the beauty of the Milky Way and other galaxies, too?

You can find other mysteries at the edge of black holes, a place known as the event horizon. Nothing that crosses this event horizon ever returns; even time itself stops inside a black hole. But we have said earlier that the universe puts nothing to waste, so where does all the material swallowed by a black hole go? Perhaps they come out very, very slowly as Hawking radiation. We don't know for sure. This is another piece of puzzle that remains to be solved by cosmic detectives like you.

The biography of the universe isn't just dry science. It is full of as many colourful stories, characters, dazzling spectacles and dark secrets as an epic movie. Less than a hundred years ago, the idea of black holes seemed to many famous scientists as science fiction or fantasy. The great Albert Einstein doubted their existence, even though his own theory had predicted them! Nature, as she often does, surprised them all. The universe turns out to be sprinkled with black holes.

You'll recall from our earlier discussion that the giant explosions caused by the death of massive stars are called supernovae, and that supernovae leave behind neutron stars and black holes. But how often do these cosmic firework shows really happen? Will you see one of them in your lifetime?

Let's take a typical bright galaxy containing 200 billion stars. In such a galaxy only about three explosions happen per century. But you know that there are at least 125 billion galaxies in our observable universe. That means 375 billion supernova explosions occur per century. Therefore, about 100 supernovae are exploding every second somewhere in the universe!

In fact, right in our own backyard, in the southern hemisphere constellation known as Carinae, a supernova is getting ready to happen. Eta Carinae, the massive star mentioned earlier in this chapter, began steadily rising in brightness again in 1940 and is in its final stages of life as a red supergiant (pic. 22). Astronomers predict that any time in the near future, it will explode and become for a time the third brightest object in the sky, after only the sun and the moon. If you live in the southern hemisphere, keep your eyes on the sky!

A special kind of supernova occurs with the participation of a white dwarf, and it is of great interest to cosmologists. If a planetary system like ours does not form during the making of a star, a pair of stars is created, orbiting one another in a cosmic waltz. This is known as a binary star. If one of the pair becomes a white dwarf, its gravity can draw matter away from its companion star like a massive vacuum cleaner, especially if the latter evolves into a red giant.

When the white dwarf has stolen enough matter from its twin such that its mass becomes 1.5 times larger than that of the sun, it explodes as a supernova. Unlike other cosmic meltdowns, however, nothing remains behind. The entire mass of the star is blown into space (pic. 21). It was the Indian-born Nobel laureate in physics, Subrahmanyam Chandrasekhar, who first hinted that such a stellar meltdown was possible, and there is a reason why scientists are especially fascinated. A characteristic light pattern radiated by this type of supernova helps them calculate precisely how far away the explosion occurred, and this in turn allows them to measure the distances of the most remote galaxies.

So, to determine the largest distances, we need the light powered by miniscule sub-atomic elements. Are you getting further hints of the relationship between the very large and very small? There is more to come.

But first, here is another investigative assignment for you. Find out what causes the recent cosmic discovery known as Gamma Ray Bursts. A hint: gamma rays are the most energetic form of light in the universe. Occasionally they are produced in very intense bursts of jets so powerful that more energy is released in few seconds than the sun would produce during its entire lifespan of 10 billion years. Do you remember that such powers are also observed during a supernova explosion arising from the death of a massive star? Could there be a connection, especially with the death of a very massive star that causes a black hole?

Now, one more assignment. We have seen that the universe wastes nothing. For each star that dies, more are born. The cosmos began to conserve and recycle long before people did. Does this mean that there has always been and always will be precisely the same amount of energy in the universe? And what is the 'power source' for the universe? Think about this as we take the next step. Be prepared. We are going to go quite a long way!

# The Runaway Universe

Detectives are often hired to find missing persons and runaways. To do this, they must determine where and how the persons came to be missing, and how much time has elapsed since their disappearance. This knowledge will tell the detective where to begin looking, and how far to search. The more time elapses since their disappearance, the further out the detective must look.

The universe, of course, isn't missing. It's right before our eyes and we are part of it. However, certain puzzle pieces of its biography—especially those depicting its birth and early moments—are missing. And it is, in a very real sense, a 'runaway'. Let me explain what I mean by that, so that together we can figure out how to pick up its trail and find the missing pieces.

Less than a century ago, even the brightest minds in science still believed that the Milky Way galaxy was all there was to the universe. Furthermore, nearly everyone regarded the universe as stable and steady. Whatever it was, scientists thought it had always been and always would be that way. No beginning, no end. But they were in for a big surprise.

Perched on a mountaintop 5,000 feet above sea level, just northeast of Los Angeles, California, is the Mt Wilson Observatory. In 1919, astronomer Edwin Hubble began watching the skies through the observatory's brand new

100-inch telescope—at that time, the most powerful in the world. Hubble's first breakthrough occurred in 1924, when he located a certain type of star called a Cepheid variable in a faint patch of light then known as the Andromeda nebula, which everyone thought was part of the Milky Way. Because their brightness varies in highly regular cycles, the actual distance of a Cepheid variable star can be calculated with great precision, and Hubble found that there was no way his star could be located within the known boundaries of the Milky Way.

No, the Andromeda nebula had to be an entirely separate galaxy, another island of stars in a universe suddenly bigger than we'd thought. We now know that Andromeda, a spiral galaxy like our own, is one of a cluster of 'neighbourhood' galaxies known as the Local Group. Its distance from the sun is roughly 2.5 million light years.

Once Hubble had identified Andromeda as a separate galaxy, others began to appear, and soon he had catalogued at least two dozens of them. With each new galaxy found, the universe got bigger. Not long after this, in 1929, he made his greatest discovery. By analysing the colour spectrum of the galaxies on his list, he found that most of the galaxies were moving rapidly away from us and from each other as well; and the further away they were, the faster they were moving.

The colour of a radiant object shifts as it moves towards and away from us, just as the tone of a train whistle or a police siren shifts as it approaches and then speeds off into the distance. If it shifts to blue, the object is getting closer. If it shifts to red, it is moving away. The colour of most of Hubble's galaxies was 'red shifted', that is they were moving away. But what could this possibly mean? Since the time people had first begun to look at the stars, they had observed that their relative positions in the night sky were basically static. Now for the first time they saw that the galaxies were rushing away from each other and that if the scientists' calculations were correct, possible galaxies out at the very edge of the observable universe might even appear to be moving with the speed of light. How could this be, and why?

The galaxies are moving apart because the universe is expanding. This is the undeniable conclusion to be drawn from Hubble's discovery, a discovery predicted by other scientists, but disbelieved until we had seen the evidence with our own eyes. It opens the secret door to the greatest mystery in cosmology, a door that all cosmic detectives eventually must walk through if they hope to complete their investigation.

Here is a fact that may take some getting used to. It will sound a little crazy at first, but remember what the great fictional detective Sherlock Holmes said, 'When you have eliminated the impossible, whatever remains, *however improbable*, must be the truth.' Now, when we think of an expanding universe, we picture the galaxies flying across empty, static space like geese flying across a winter sky. But this is not what is happening. It is space itself that is expanding, and carrying the galaxies with it.

Wait just a minute! Isn't space simply a whole lot of nothing? How can 'nothing' expand? The answer is that space is not nothing. There are two ways to picture the expansion of the universe. Neither one is precisely accurate, but they will give you a place to start. If you can get your hands on a wide rubber band—the kind that's used to wrap big Sunday newspapers—cut it with a pair of scissors and lay it flat on a table. Take a pen and draw ten or twelve vertical lines on the rubber band. Each of the vertical lines represents a galaxy. Then take hold of both ends and stretch the rubber band. You'll see that the vertical lines have moved apart, because the rubber band (space) has expanded. You can do pretty much the same demonstration with a balloon. Blow it up halfway and, with a felt tip marker, make a few tight clusters of dots (stars) in the shape of galaxies. Then blow the balloon up fully and observe what has happened. The surface of the balloon represents space, and space is expanding.

The true expansion of the universe is a little harder to imagine. We'll have to depict the galaxies and clusters of galaxies moving apart in three dimensions of space and one of time. They would not lie only on the surface of the balloon, and as one galaxy sped past us, another would appear behind it, and on and on and on. In this case, the surface of the balloon would represent the 'edge' of the universe, nearly 14 billion years old. And here is the spooky part. When a balloon is blown up, it expands into the existing space around it. But there is no 'existing space' outside the universe. The universe *is* cloning space between galaxies as it expands. That is to say, it is making new space where no space was before.

All of this brings up some very big questions. If the universe is expanding, what is it expanding from, and where is it going? These are exactly the questions that science asked in the wake of Edwin Hubble's discovery, and some very bright scientists were prepared with ideas. We are going to examine their ideas towards the end of our investigation, but first we have some fieldwork to do.

We have only begun to cover the ground our runaway universe has travelled. A detective's case must be built up by the gathering of physical evidence, piece by piece; only then will his conclusion be supported by the facts. When you have reviewed the evidence, you may reach the same inference the great minds of science did. But you are the detective, and you must come to it on your own.

As we make our survey of the universe near and far, however, the facts discovered almost a hundred years ago bear keeping in mind. The universe is in motion. The space we will traverse in our investigation is a something, not a nothing. It can be bent, folded, warped, and maybe even tunnelled through! All of this was predicted by Einstein's famous Theory of Relativity, and most of it has now been proven by observation.

What is this space filled with, how did it come to be filled, how big is it, and how did we come along to ask these questions? When your mind begins to get boggled by the enormity of it all, it will help to remember that in the universe, what is true in the near is usually true in the far; what is true of the small is often true of the large. Try not to be intimidated by the distances and sizes involved. In a sense, the universe is right around the corner!

What exactly is a 'universe'? Why that word and not another? 'Uni' means one, from the Latin *unus*, and 'verse' is derived from the Latin *vertere*: to turn. In other words, the universe 'turns as one'. And despite its many peculiarities and unknowns, the universe does seem to be a remarkably consistent place. Another way to look at it is to consider 'verse' in the way we currently use it: as something sung or recited in rhythm. And the universe truly is like an epic poem. Nowhere is it out of rhyme. It is fair to say that on the large scale, everything in this universe is evolving in concert with everything else. This is remarkable, considering how enormously big it is.

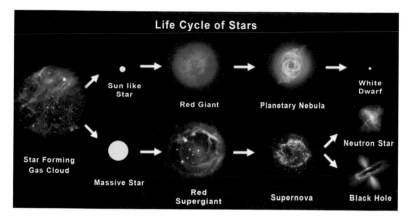

**Life Cycle of Stars**

Star Forming Gas Cloud

Sun like Star

Red Giant

Planetary Nebula

White Dwarf

Massive Star

Red Supergiant

Supernova

Neutron Star

Black Hole

15. Illustration of the life cycle of stars.

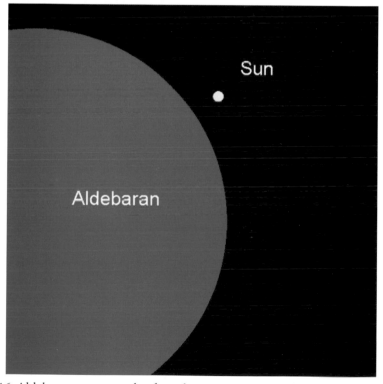

16. Aldebaran, an example of a red giant. You can see that its size is vast compared to our Sun. About 5 billion years from now, our Sun will become a red giant before its death. Earth will be engulfed by the giant fireball and be destroyed. Before that we need to find our new address somewhere else in the universe, in a planet like Earth.

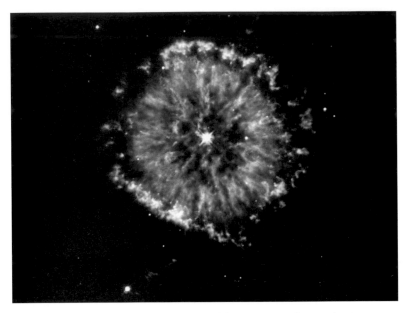

17. The Glowing Eye nebula looking like gorgeous fireworks in space. The associated white dwarf star is visible in its centre.

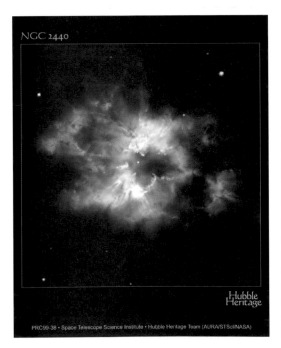

NGC 2440

18. The gas and dust thrown out by a red giant at the end of its life created this planetary nebula. The remainder of the star, a white dwarf of higher temperature, is visible near the centre. Our Sun will also die this way about 5 billion years from now.

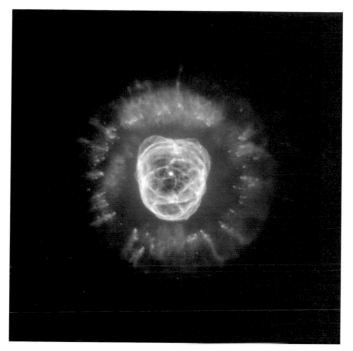

19. The Eskimo planetary nebula looks like another beautiful firework in space. Its associated white dwarf is again visible in the centre.

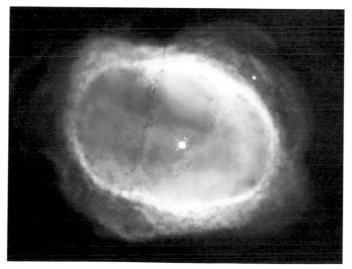

20. Another one of the beautiful planetary nebula: NGC 3132.

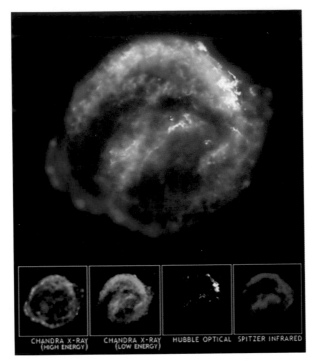

CHANDRA X-RAY (HIGH ENERGY)   CHANDRA X-RAY (LOW ENERGY)   HUBBLE OPTICAL   SPITZER INFRARED

21. The Kepler supernova that exploded in 1604. This is a compound image made from photographs taken by X-ray to infrared radiations; this type of supernova leaves nothing at its core. No supernova has been visually observed in our galaxy since then. However, occurrence of recent supernovae that are obscured by the gas and dust of the Milky Way is now seen in X-ray and radio images.

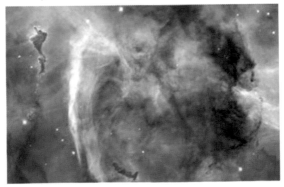

22. Eta Carinae, a star about 150 times more massive than our Sun, has produced this beautiful gas cloud even before its explosion as a supernova. Recently, an enormous, spontaneous ultraviolet laser has been located in this gas cloud, which harbours a red supergiant.

23. A small portion of the Orion nebula, created by the accumulation of gas and dust from many stellar explosions, looks like a gorgeous abstract painting in space.

24. The Crab nebula consists of the material blown out by a supernova that was so bright that it could be seen even in the daytime. Chinese astronomers wrote about it on July 4, 1054 AD.

25. Indication of a neutron star, like a spinning top, at the core of the Crab nebula.

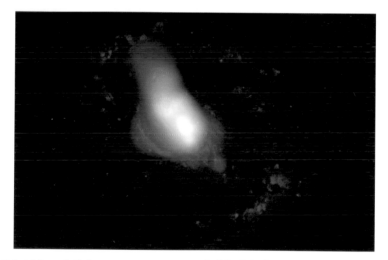

26. Although light cannot come out of a black hole, the rotating infalling matter gets very hot before it disappears in the black hole. The rotating disc creates a very strong magnetic field that ejects some of the infalling matter with very high speed into a narrow jet. The bubble seen in the picture is from the light emitted by the jet when it collides with the surrounding cold gas. By analysing the speed of rotation of the disc, scientists can calculate with confidence that masses of billions of stars could be packed in a black hole. Black holes are believed to reside at the centre of most bright galaxies.

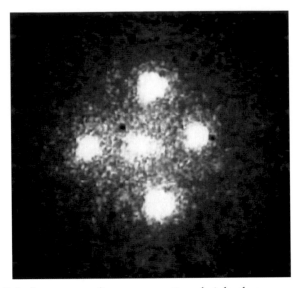

27. The light from a very distant quasar is so bright that we can see it as a star from billions of light years away. The multiple images of this single quasar are produced by the passage of its light through an intervening galaxy located between Earth and the quasar. Einstein's theory can explain this pattern very well.

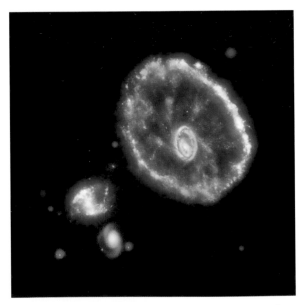

28. Example of an irregular galaxy formed by the collision of two galaxies.

How big? It is really difficult even to imagine. A basic measuring stick in the universe is the astronomical unit, or AU, the distance between the earth and the sun. This distance is just under 93 million miles or 150 million kilometres. Light can travel that distance in minutes, but unless we can figure out a way to ride on a beam of light, it will take you and me a very long time to cover it. Pluto, the distant dwarf planet in our solar system, is forty AUs from the sun! Imagine how cold it is that far away from the sun.

Once we have left our neighbourhood in space, astronomical units are not much good as a measure of distance. We must speak in terms of how far light can travel in a year, which as we have seen is about 6 trillion miles. Do you know how to write a trillion? If you put six zeroes after 1 (1,000,000) you get a million, nine zeroes after 1 (1,000,000,000) gives us a billion, and twelve zeroes after 1 (1,000,000,000,000) makes a trillion. To give you an idea of just how large a number this is, if you were to count one star per second, it would take 11.5 days to count a million stars, 31.7 years to count a billion of them, and 31,700 years for a trillion!

Let's put it in terms of speed. Light travels at 186,282 miles per second. How fast is that? If you could run at the speed of light, you could reach the moon in about 1.3 second. In a car running at 75 miles per hour, it will take you about 133 days, but 9 million years to cover the 6 trillion miles that light can travel in a year. 9 million years and we have not even made it to the nearest star!

If we are to describe the size of the universe, not even one light year is adequate. When we reach galactic proportions, scientists must use an even larger measure. The centre of the Milky Way is about 26,000 light years from earth, and our galaxy itself is about 100,000 light years across. This doesn't even begin to map the cosmos as a whole. To reach the farthest galaxies, we need measures like million or billion light years.

Are you feeling a little lonely in this vast universe? Then let's find out who our neighbours are. Is there another sun-like star near our own? Yes, indeed. It is Proxima Centauri, 4.2 light years away from us. A hop, skip, and a jump in cosmic terms, but still a long way to go in a spaceship. Our nearest large galactic neighbour, you may recall, is Andromeda. You will find it only 2.5 million light years away.

There is an interesting fact about the Andromeda galaxy. We learned earlier in this chapter how Edwin Hubble showed that most of the galaxies were moving apart because their colour was red shifted. Andromeda, however, is blue shifted with respect to us. That means it's moving closer! The Milky Way and Andromeda are part of a local group of galaxies. Because of their strong mutual gravitational attraction, they move towards each other in a local scale even though the group as a whole is part of the runaway universe.

Scientists estimate that in about 3.5 billion years—somewhat earlier than the time our sun begins to burn out—the Milky Way and Andromeda galaxies will collide with each other. Their spiral arms will pass through each other, stirring up enormous streams of gas and dust. The spectacle will take millions of years to unfold and leave a multitude of new stars in the sky for whoever is lucky enough to be around to see them!

The size, distance, form and distribution of galaxies are very important clues to the ultimate mysteries of the universe. By studying this evidence, we gather information about what kind of 'seeds' formed them, and the special features of these seeds can tell us a great deal about the moment of creation of the universe.

We now know that galaxies don't travel alone. They are arranged throughout the universe in clusters, super clusters, and even larger units called filaments, lined up—in the words of one astronomer—like sparkling beads on a string. The Milky Way galaxy and its local group are part of the Virgo super cluster, but there are still larger structures like the 500-million-light-years long Great Wall, located 200 million light years away from us. What happened in the early universe that caused them to clump this way, and why do they remain clumped despite the expansion of space? What holds them together?

As a cosmic detective, I am sure, you have many queries. Let me answer some of them for you. How far is the most distant galaxy we can observe from earth? It is nearly 45 billion light years away, near the very edge of the visible universe. Put another way, light from that galaxy—streaming towards us at a speed of 186,286 miles per second—takes nearly the age of the universe to reach us. But during that time the galaxy itself has moved further away due to the expansion of the universe. Try as we might, we can never catch up with it.

Were there real galaxies 13 billion years ago? We have proof of their existence by observation through the Hubble Space Telescope. Observing the oldest stars, scientists estimate that our own Milky Way galaxy has been in business for at least 12 billion years. There may be elements of stardust in you and I which are that old. If only stardust could remember, we could glimpse where we come from!

Why are the stars not ejected from the spinning galaxies like contestants on *Indian Idol*? Because, the gravitational attraction of the galaxy keeps them inside. This is the force we encountered during our investigation of the life cycle of the stars and it is this force that keeps things from flying apart.

To wrap up our review of the galaxies, before making closer surveys, we have discovered three types: elliptical, irregular and spiral. About 80 per cent of the galaxies we observe are elliptical. Elliptical galaxies, true to their name, are shaped like an elongated sphere (pic. 30). Most ellipticals are small in comparison to the bright spirals. Ellipticals are home to stars much older than those in the Milky Way, and since they have used up most of their supply of dust and gas, not much new star making goes on there. They are 'worn out', and as a result, not very bright, but they have done their service for the universe.

Irregular galaxies come in two types. The first type results from the collision of two galaxies (pics. 28, 31) and is rather large. The second type is smaller, and probably created by the distortion of matter, which occurs when galaxies interact during close encounters in their journeys! The inside of an irregular galaxy does not have an identifiable pattern, nor is there a true centre. There is, however, plenty of gas and dust in these galaxies, and that makes them good places for the production of new stars.

The vast majority of bright, active galaxies we can observe are spirals, and we have already spent some time examining this type. A huge amount of molecular gas and dust resides in the arms of spiral galaxies, and as these arms sweep space in their ceaseless revolution about the galactic centre, new stars in the universe are born at least a thousand times as often as babies are born on earth!

The distance across a galaxy can be as few as 1,000 or as many as 300,000 light years. The number of stars in a galaxy is typically over a billion, but can be as many as 1 trillion. Just as nations on earth consist of small villages, larger towns, and big cities, the 'nation' of the cosmos incorporates galactic 'population centres' of many different sizes. How distant from one another are the large galaxies? At least 500,000 light years away. And what fills the vast stretches of space between them? We will see.

There was once a time on earth when the land between cities was covered by great fields and forests. In space, this open country consists mostly of a very low density ionized gas called plasma. Because of the vastness of the universe, the plasma consists of 75 per cent of the ordinary matter that you and I are made of. But there are more exotic substances lurking out there, too. Let us not forget the mysterious dark matter and dark energy we mentioned earlier. These require some serious detective work, and may help solve the case of the runaway universe. Here, you and the scientists will be companions, because they are as much 'in the dark' as you are!

Let's take a long-view look at the Milky Way from our place in it. We already know that the earth orbits our sun; the sun in turn orbits the centre of our galaxy. The earth takes one year to go once around the sun. The sun—and all its planets—make one revolution of the Milky Way in 220 million years. And we're not the only ones making this circuit. We have credible proof of the existence of over 300 other planetary systems in our galaxy alone. Convincing signs of a planetary atmosphere has been found in at least one of them. What is true here is also likely to be true elsewhere. As wild, violent and unpredictable as the universe can be, we find that on the large scale its features are indeed more alike than different.

We are members of the sun family, and if we encounter intelligent creatures from another solar system some day, we may introduce ourselves this way. Just as people once identified themselves as belonging, for example, to the Kalika tribe from the desert on the far side of the Blue Mountains, we may describe our 'tribe' as coming from the yellow sun with eight planets in the sector of Orion. That's as good a reason as any to familiarize ourselves with our part of the universe.

Before we do that, here is another challenge for you. We have learned that when we look out into deep space, we are also looking back in time. Could this point us to where the universe began? And if we decide to follow this trail, what will we learn about ourselves?

# Our Solar Family

Travel with me for a moment to a lonely place about 80 AU—that's more than 7 billion miles—from the centre of our solar system. Out here, the Sun is a distant lamp in the darkness of space, and its rays take nearly eleven hours to reach us. Did I remind you to bring a very warm coat? It's really cold out here! Our home planet Earth is just a speck of reflected sunlight, making its yearly course around the Sun, and even if we could text message our friends to let them know where we are, it would take quite a while to receive a reply.

At first, we see nothing but emptiness around us. The nearest planet is a few billion miles away. Our loneliness is deeper than anything we have ever experienced. Then, suddenly, a tiny, moving object appears on our left, its shell reflecting the long-travelled sunlight and bearing the letters NASA. It is the spacecraft known as Pioneer 10, and it left the earth in 1972. Its fuel is gone and its batteries have run down, but it continues on its outward journey. If we hitched a ride, we'd end up very far away indeed.

As distant as we are from the Sun, we have not reached the outermost shores of our solar system. We are now past the area known as the Kuiper Belt. Objects out there still feel the gravitational attraction of our star and orbit around it.

And what sort of objects are they? Dirty snowballs—clumps of packed ice and rocks of various sizes, some of them nearly as big as a thousand kilometres across (or the size of the state of Rajasthan!).

These are the leftovers from the creation of our solar system, and by examining them, we can begin to see how Earth and the other planets formed long ago from that rotating cloud of gas and dust that gave birth to the Sun. If one of these giant snowballs were to be nudged out of orbit, it would head straight for the Sun and become known as a comet. The Kuiper Belt is one of the two places in the solar system from which comets begin their journey. We'll visit the other place shortly, but now, let's leave this cold, lonely outpost behind and head back towards the blazing centre of things.

## The Sun and its Family

The Sun is our solar family's head of household and provider. Most importantly for us, there would be no life without it. So, it's easy to understand why our ancestors worshipped it, built temples in its honour and made sacrifices to it. They figured out fairly quickly that things die without the warmth and light of the Sun.

How can a star warm us from 93 million miles away? Remember that the temperature at the Sun's surface—called the photosphere—is an average 6,093 degrees Centigrade (C) or 11,000 degrees Fahrenheit (F), and that at the centre of its dense core, the heat comes from about 15 million degrees C (27 million degrees F)! That warmth rides the solar radiation to you and me, and by the time it reaches Earth, the temperature is just right for sustaining life. We know that this heat is produced mainly by the nuclear fusion of hydrogen, and we have examined how stars like the Sun are born and how, finally, they die. We have also learned that the planets in our solar system were formed in the same primal protostar disc that produced the Sun.

There are eight principal planets (pic. 33) and several 'dwarf planets' orbiting our Sun. You probably know their names already, but you may not know their personalities, and like all siblings, each one is different. The nearest to the Sun is Mercury. Then comes Venus. The third planet from the Sun is our Earth and beyond Earth lie Mars, Jupiter, Saturn, Uranus and Neptune, and finally—40 AU from the centre of the solar system—the little dwarf planet Pluto.

Most of the planets, in turn, have families of their own. We have seen that what is true of the universe on the large scale is often true on the small, and just as the planets revolve around the Sun, all but two of them—Mercury and Venus—have moons that revolve around them. You may have heard the expression 'a chip off the old block', used to describe a child who resembles his parent. Well, the planetary moons are literally 'chips off the old block', since they were made mostly from chunks of the same raw material as the planet aeons ago. Planet Earth has one moon, Mars has two. Then their number jumps to sixty-three for Jupiter and fifty-six for Saturn. Uranus has twenty-seven moons, and Neptune, thirteen. Even Pluto, though far smaller than Earth, has three moons which have been identified so far. So, the number of moons in the solar family is 165.

Let's pay a visit to each of the Sun's planetary associates, beginning with the one nearest to its fire. And remember: whatever we learn of the planets in our own solar system is in general likely to be true of other systems in other parts of the galaxy and the cosmos. We are not the only game in town!

## MERCURY

The planet closest to the Sun, at an average distance of 36 million miles or 58 million kilometres, is Mercury (pic. 34). By astronomical standards, that's right next door, and Mercury feels the full blast of the Sun's heat. Daytime temperatures reach 450 degrees C or 840 degrees F. You and I would roast in a matter of minutes! On the other hand, the night-time temperature drops to minus 170 degrees C or minus 275 degrees F. You may ask why Mercury is a place of such extreme temperatures. It is because the length of a day or a night on Mercury is as long as three Earth months. During its long nights, it does not receive any sunlight and there is almost no atmosphere to trap the previous day's heat.

A year on Mercury is shorter than its one day because the planet orbits the Sun faster than it can spin on its axis. One year on Mercury equals 88 Earth days, while the interval between sunrise to sunrise is 176 Earth days.

Mercury is small and slightly less dense than Earth, with a solid iron core the size of our moon. Its surface is covered with large craters and many wrinkled ridges. It is a harsh and hostile planet, and if we're looking for another planet to settle when the Earth no longer has room for all of us, we'll have to look elsewhere.

## VENUS

We won't be vacationing on Venus any time soon either, even though it has almost exactly the same size, internal structure and chemical makeup as Earth. Its atmosphere is a choking, smoggy mixture of carbon dioxide and thick, fast-moving clouds (pic. 35) suffused with deadly sulphuric acid, making it the hottest planet in the solar system—as hot as 482 degrees C or 900 degrees F. A long time ago, some people believed that Venus might have been a kind of tropical paradise, but we now know better. Some scientists have called it Earth's evil twin, but to poets Venus has long been known as the Morning Star. It is the third brightest object in the sky after the Sun and the moon and is also known as the Evening Star.

Its orbit lies between those of Mercury and Earth, about 67 million miles or 108 million kilometres from the Sun. No other planet's orbit brings it nearer to us. Venus comes within about 23.7 million miles or 38.2 million kilometres of Earth at its closest approach. One year on Venus—the time it takes to orbit the Sun—is equal to 225 Earth days, but because it spins so slowly, one Venusian day is 243 of ours! And not only does it spin slowly, it spins backwards, that is, in the opposite direction of Earth. This is what is known as a retrograde rotation. On Venus, the Sun rises in the west and sets in the east. Use your detective skills to make a guess as to why this might be.

The acid cloud that covers Venus is driven around it by hurricane winds with speeds up to 220 miles per hour. It never rains, but the Venusian sky is filled with thunder and lightning most of the time. The atmospheric pressure on its surface (pic. 36) is about ninety times greater than that on Earth. All in all, the planet named by the Romans after the romantic goddess of love is not a great place for honeymoon!

## EARTH

The third planet from the Sun, at an average distance of 92,957,000 miles or 149,600,000 kilometres, is our own Earth.

It is the largest and densest of the so-called terrestrial rocky planets (Mercury, Venus, Earth and Mars), and so far as we know, the only one which has been able to support life. The Earth orbits the Sun in 365 days, which is, of course, the length of our year, and takes twenty-four hours to make one rotation on its axis, from one sunrise to another, and that is the length of our day.

The average temperature on Earth is 15 degrees C or 59 degrees F—the temperature of a spring day—although it has recently been getting a bit warmer. Most scientists believe that this warming is the result of the accumulation of so-called greenhouse gases in our atmosphere, with many potentially worrisome long-term effects. But of all the members of the Sun's family, our Earth is by far the most beautiful, quiet and pleasant. There is more water than land mass on the surface of Earth. From space, we can see (pic. 37) fluffy clouds surround our planet, floating in an atmosphere that consists mostly of nitrogen and oxygen that protects us from the most harmful radiations streaming to Earth. How is it that our Earth got so lucky?

The age of Earth is nearly 4.5 billion years, just like the other members of the solar family. At its beginning, the newly created Earth looked quite different from what it is today. There were no fluffy white clouds in blue skies, no blue oceans, no green forests, and no beautiful moonlit nights. In fact, the moon did not even exist. Shortly after its birth in the protoplanetary solar disc, an object possibly as big as a small planet collided with Earth and knocked a chunk of it loose. That chunk became our moon. Why do we believe this? Because the chemical composition of the moon is quite similar to that of Earth's outer mantle. Neither Earth nor the moon was round in the beginning. Have you noticed that the longer an object spins, the rounder it becomes? Why do you suppose this is, and where did the massive object that crashed into Earth come from, to set the moon free?

The Moon is a great beacon in our night sky, and the subject of countless poems and love songs. But its effect is more than figurative: the tides on Earth are caused mainly by the moon's gravitational attraction. And as the solid surface of Earth rotates through the 'tidal bulge', a friction is generated that slows down the rotation minutely. Such is the effect of one heavenly body on another!

This causes the length of the day on Earth to increase slightly and as it does, the moon gradually recedes from Earth. The cumulative effect of this minute change can become significant over many years. 4 billion years ago, the moon was much less distant from Earth than it is now; and at that time, one day on Earth was possibly only about six hours long, as opposed to twenty-four hours today! A year, on the other hand, would have lasted about 1,500 days. Of course, humans weren't around 4 billion years ago, but can you see how it would have affected our lives?

The anticipated temperature on Earth in its early days was even hotter than that of Venus today. Lava and gas erupted from its core. The gases coming out with this volcanic turmoil created the atmosphere. The primal atmosphere on Earth consisted of nitrogen, carbon dioxide, carbon monoxide and water vapour, along with some methane and ammonia. The water vapour gradually made Earth suitable for the emergence of life. As the vapours rose from the surface, they cooled and formed clouds, then returned to Earth as rain. Earth was so hot that this process occurred continually for some time.

Eventually the rain was soaked up by rocks on the

surface, and when the rocks became saturated, the water began to gather in large craters. This is how the oceans were formed. As the seas grew larger and deeper, the sky became thinner, and the Sun shone brightly on the water.

While water accumulated in the oceans, the land masses were shaping and reshaping. The continents as we now see them did not exist on primitive Earth, but were joined together as various super continents which formed and broke down over billions of years. The last such super continent is known as Pangaea, and it began to break apart 200 million years ago, splitting into two distinct parts 65 million years later. The northern part was Laurasia and the southern part Gondwanaland. These pieces in turn broke down to become the continents that we see on the map today. As the land masses slipped on Earth's surface, the floor of the oceans was also transformed. You might be surprised to learn that the longest mountain range on Earth is under the sea. It is called the Mid Oceanic Ridge, and some of its peaks rise above the surface of the ocean. One such peak is Iceland.

Earth is a little like an apple. The outer layer of Earth, which is about forty kilometres deep, is called the crust and is like an apple's skin. Beneath the crust is the mantle, about 2,900 kilometres thick, like the meat of the apple. The outer core of liquid iron is conventionally taken to extend from 2,900 kilometres to 5,150 kilometres beneath the surface of the planet and creates Earth's magnetic field. The innermost core is a solid sphere of nearly a 2,500-kilometre diameter and made of iron with a little bit of nickel. Although the temperature of the core can reach up to 5,000 degrees C, it remains solid under very high pressure.

Most scientists believe that the seed of life first sprouted on Earth about 3.5 billion years ago, but not on land. Our most distant ancestors were simple life forms like bacteria that lived in the ocean. These tiny 'creatures' evolved over a period of several hundred million years into life forms such as blue-green algae, which were able to make their own food with the aid of sunlight and chlorophyll in a process called photosynthesis. Sugar (or glucose) was made from carbon dioxide and water, providing energy for their sustenance and creating oxygen as a by-product. It was this oxygen that allowed the higher life forms to evolve.

Plants first grew under water and gradually came to the surface, forming a vast green panorama. Fish appeared in the water about 475 million years ago, followed by the age of reptiles 225 million years ago. Dinosaurs were the most impressive of the reptiles, and ruled Earth for over 150 million years. The age of dinosaurs came to an end 65 million years ago, and it is now believed that the effects of an asteroid (pic. 44) impact—possibly near the Yucatan Peninsula of Mexico—were responsible for their extinction.

The age of mammals came next, with humans eventually becoming the leaders, but the age of reptiles continued as a separate tier, just as the humble bacterium and algae continued. From a rough estimate, scientists tell us that there are 1.4 million different animal species and 500,000 species of plants present on Earth today, all producing—and consuming—the planet's resources.

An important fact to remember is that 90 per cent of all species to have evolved on Earth are now extinct. Only those species able to adapt themselves to the changing environment remain. Penguins and sharks are both examples of survivors: species that have continued to live on Earth for 200 million years.

However, life abides on Earth even in the most inhospitable places. Salt lakes, hot mineral springs, deep oceans, the top of the atmosphere, or on top of ice—life can be supported everywhere on the planet. Our Earth, alone among the members of the solar family, is a haven for life. Life blossoms in its air, water, mountains and rainforests. In fact, life is hard to avoid anywhere on Earth. Could life exist elsewhere in the solar system, at least in a rudimentary form? You can join the others who are busy looking for it.

## MARS

The fourth member of the solar family and the outermost of the rocky planets is Mars, 141,700,000 miles or 228,000,000 kilometres from the Sun. One year on Mars consists of 687 Earth days, while a Martian day is very much like ours: twenty-four hours and thirty-seven minutes. Mars has two moons, potato-shaped Phobos (which may be a captured asteroid) and Deimos. Mars (pic. 38) also has summer and winter seasons, but not like those on Earth. The temperature on Mars does not rise above the freezing point even in summer, and the land remains permanently frozen the rest of the time. Storms of red dust whipped up by strong Martian winds rage across its surface frequently. It would be a harsh place for a human settler, a little like the Arctic. But humans do live in the Arctic, and humans could live on Mars as well.

For more than a hundred years there has been talk of the possibility of life on Mars. Why? The answer lies in one word: water. We can see frozen water on the planet's polar areas, and even on the dry Martian surface, there are features (pics. 41, 43) that appear to have been formed by once free-flowing water. There is strong evidence that Mars once had lakes and even floods of water. If this was the case, then aeons ago when perhaps the climate was not so hostile, could there have been life there? Could there still be? One day we will have the answer, because one day man will walk—maybe even live—on the red planet. One of you may go there, and if you do, look for fingerprints!

Where did the water of Mars go? Much of it probably vaporized and escaped through the thin Martian atmosphere, but we can say with some confidence that there is plenty of water confined below the surface or in the polar caps in the form of ice.

The largest known volcano in the solar system is on Mars. It is called Olympus Mons (pic. 42) and is 370 miles wide and 16 miles high—three times higher than Mt Everest. It is no longer an active volcano, but once was.

Why is Mars red? Because the dust (pic. 40) covering the planet contains quite a bit of iron oxide. Iron oxide is otherwise known as rust, and that's why Mars looks reddish from a distance. The chemical composition of the stones on Mars, however, is generally quite similar to those on Earth.

An international effort to make Mars habitable for a human colony is being contemplated. Because of the severe dust storms, this colony would have to be underground, but if science has conceived it, it will almost surely happen. The planet named after the Roman god of war may be our future big real-estate bonanza (pic. 39). Will you one day purchase ten acres there?

## ASTEROIDS AND METEOROIDS

Between the orbits of Mars and Jupiter are several hundred thousand multi-sized chunks of rock, orbiting the Sun on their own timetables. This is the Asteroid Belt, and it is believed to be the material for a planet that never formed.

An asteroid can be as big as a small moon or as small as a dust particle. According to the new terminology of astronomy, asteroids are now called small solar system bodies. Although large in number, they are spread over such a vast swath of space that no spacecraft in its journey through the region has ever collided with an asteroid.

On 12 February 2001, the NEAR space probe (Near Earth Asteroid Rendezvous) came to a soft landing on a large asteroid known as 433 Eros. There were no astronauts on board, but imagine if there had been! They might have felt a bit like the character in the French children's tale, *The Little Prince*. NEAR confirmed that asteroids are solid object, and cratered like the moon from their violent history.

The Asteroid Belt begins 50 million miles away from Mars and extends for more than 100 million miles towards the orbit of Jupiter. During the formative age of the solar system, Mercury, Venus and Mars, as well as our Earth, were frequently hit by wayward asteroids and comets. Except for Earth—now covered by oceans and vegetation—the signs of cosmic bombing are still to be seen on the surface of these planets. But Earth has been hit and will likely be hit again. It's comforting to know that the mission of NEAR showed that we may one day be able to divert an asteroid that appears to be on a collision course with Earth.

The first asteroid was identified in 1801 by Giuseppe Piazzi, and is called Ceres. It is the largest asteroid we have observed, and by the new definition is now called a dwarf planet. Since then, other large asteroids such as Pallas, Juno, and Vesta have been discovered. But even if we were to glue all the asteroids together, the resulting object would be smaller than the moon.

Some small asteroids get knocked out of their orbit and wind up on their trajectory towards Earth. These are called meteoroids. If they enter our atmosphere, we label them meteors, and most are small enough to burn up from friction with the atmosphere before ever reaching the planet. Streaking across the night sky like fiery messengers, we know them as shooting stars. If they happen to land in our backyard, we call them meteorites. If you find one, keep it. It's evidence of how the solar system came to be, and will be useful in your investigation.

Occasionally, a large asteroid wanders quite close to Earth. The asteroid known as Hermes came within 300,000 miles or 480,000 kilometres of us, a distance roughly equal to that of the moon. In July 2006 another asteroid—as large as half a mile across—also came as close to Earth as Hermes did. A collision with an asteroid of this size would do great damage. How much damage? The equivalent of 20,000 one megaton hydrogen bombs exploding at the same time. But we needn't worry that such an object will strike Earth any time soon. The odds are strongly in our favour since these events happen only once in 65 to 100 million years. And even if it did, soon we will have the technology to divert them safely away from Earth.

## JUPITER

We now leave the region of the rocky planets and enter the realm of the gas giants, planets with solid cores but without solid surfaces. We could not walk, ride a bicycle or drive a car on these members of the solar family. Jupiter, the fifth planet from the Sun and the largest of the gas giants, is thought to be a failed star, one whose mass never became great enough to trigger nuclear fusion. That failure, however, did not keep Jupiter from being the biggest planet in the solar system. So big, in fact, that all the other planets and their satellites could fit inside it. Its mass is about 2.5 times greater than the combined mass of the other planets.

King Jupiter orbits the Sun at a distance of 483,700,000 miles or 778,400,000 kilometres, rotating so quickly on its axis (once every nine hours, fifty-six minutes as compared to our Earth's twenty-four hours) that its atmosphere is swept into bands of colour which give the planet a striped appearance (pic. 45). Although its day is short, its year is equal to 11.86 of Earth's. And Jupiter, befitting its size and status, has more moons than any other planet: sixty-three at last count! The largest (pic. 47) four—Io, Europa, Ganymede and Callisto—were first observed and named by Galileo in January 1610. Ganymede alone has a diameter greater than that of the planet Mercury.

Although Jupiter is mostly gaseous, its moons are solid, rocky bodies, like the terrestrial planets, each one with its own personality. Io (pic. 48), for instance, is the most volcanically active place in the solar system. Europa (pic. 49) may have an ocean of liquid water flowing beneath its cracked, icy surface, and as we have seen, where there is liquid water, there is the possibility of life. Hence, scientists are looking closely at Europa.

Here is a question to add to your investigative file: is there any reason why only planets like Earth should harbour life? Why not moons? And if Jupiter has at least sixty-three of them, there's a lot of ground to cover!

Jupiter is a dramatic, stormy place. When the Galileo spacecraft began sending information back from Jupiter in 1995, it measured wind speeds of 330 mph and gusts of as much as 1,000 mph. Thunderclaps and jagged bolts of lightning shake and sear Jupiter's turbulent atmosphere. Unlike storm systems on Earth, the turbulent storms of Jupiter are believed to be powered by its internal heat. This is supported by the fact that Jupiter radiates more energy than it receives from the Sun.

The largest storm system of all is highlighted by what is known as the Great Red Spot, a persistent turbulence five miles high and three times as wide as Earth. It's no picnic on the largest planet in our solar system, so plan your vacation for one of Jupiter's moons instead.

Astronomers have observed that the great Jupiter is surrounded by at least three rings (pic. 46) that formed when dust from its nearest moons was tossed up into space. These rings, however, cannot rival those of our next family member.

## SATURN

If there is one planet other than Earth that everyone can recognize instantly, it is the sixth member of the solar family, Saturn. Although we now know that Jupiter, Uranus and Neptune also have rings surrounding them, none is as spectacular or beautiful (pic. 51) as Saturn's. To reach this mysterious, ringed planet, we would have to travel 886,700,000 miles or 1,427,000,000 kilometres from the Sun, so far from the centre of the solar system that one year on Saturn is equal to 29.46 Earth years. By that measure, none of you has been born yet! Or take the example of a man who dies on Earth at the age of sixty: in Saturn years, he would have died when he was only two years old.

Galileo spotted Saturn's magnificent rings in 1610, but

his telescope was not sharp enough to resolve them well. To him they appeared as two matching ears, or cup handles, one on each side of the planet. In 1659, the Dutch astronomer Christiaan Huygens theorized that Saturn was a world surrounded by rings solid enough to use as a racetrack, but by the mid-eighteenth century, scientists had determined that Saturn's rings were made of ice, rock and dust. We now know that the rings are formed of billions of ice particles mixed with rock and silicates, some as small as a grain of sand while others as big as three feet in diameter. The major rings of Saturn are extremely wide. The outer ring alone may be as much as 186,000 miles wide or 300,000 kilometres. The rings form a thin disc that circles Saturn's mid-section.

Not all scientists agree about how these rings came to be, but a likely guess seems to be that they were formed when a collision of one of Saturn's moons with a comet threw out an enormous quantity of dust particles, which were then aligned in obedience to Saturn's gravitational force.

Saturn (pic. 50) has at least fifty-six known moons, of which the largest is Titan (pic. 52). Titan is of special interest to us because a visit by the Voyager 2 spacecraft in 1981 revealed that the composition of its atmosphere—nitrogen, argon, methane and other gases—was similar to that of Earth 4 billion years ago. An investigation of Titan could therefore give us some clues about what Earth was like in its earliest days. The big difference between Titan and Earth is in the atmospheric temperature: Titan is so cold that higher forms of life would find it almost impossible to develop there. Otherwise, Titan is more similar to Earth than any other member of the solar family, and thus an excellent place to spend a few days of detective work.

There's another interesting fact about Titan. Its atmosphere is as thick as that of Earth, but the gravitational attraction on its surface is only 14 per cent of that on Earth. On Titan, you could fly like a bird with the help of some wings.

Like Jupiter (and just a little smaller in size), Saturn is a gas giant and its moons (pics. 50, 52, 53) are solid and rocky. Saturn is a bit less turbulent than Jupiter, but from time to time it experiences great storms which form the coloured bands in its atmosphere.

## URANUS

To greet the seventh member of the solar family, we'll have to travel 1.784 billion miles or 2.871 billion kilometres from the Sun, and it is beginning to get very cold out here! The temperature at the top of Uranus's icy clouds of methane gas is about minus 215 degrees C or minus 355 degrees F. Like Jupiter and Saturn, Uranus is a gas giant with a rocky core but no solid surface. The fastest wind speed on Uranus is as high as 450 mph or 724 kilometres per hour.

The eleven rings (pic. 55) of Uranus we have observed so far are composed of rock particles and dust, and are less reflective than those of Saturn. Uranus orbits the Sun in 84.01 Earth years, which means that you'd celebrate your first birthday here at the age of eighty-four!

The oddest feature of Uranus is its extremely tilted rotational axis, possibly the consequence of a collision ages ago which rocked the planet out of kilter. As a result, Uranus looks like a gigantic bowling ball rolling on its side during a part of its journey around the Sun.

We learned of our seventh family member in 1781, when it was discovered by Sir William Herschel. Herschel, an Englishman, named the moons of Uranus (those he was able to identify) after characters from Shakespeare. Among them are Miranda, Ariel, Umbriel, Titania and Oberon, the most prominent moons of Uranus. So far we have observed twenty-seven moons in all, each of them just as solid and rocky as Earth.

In 1986, the Voyager 2 spacecraft passed by Uranus and informed us that its atmosphere was rich in methane. Sunlight scattered from the clouds surrounding Uranus is reflected back through these methane layers, giving this planet—the third largest in our solar system—its blue-green colour (pic. 54).

As with all of the planets (and many of the stars), the name of the seventh planet has a mythological origin. The Roman god Uranus was father of Saturn and grandfather of Jupiter, and the orbits of these three generations of the solar family fall in exactly this order.

Seen from Uranus, the Sun appears as a very bright star, but not nearly as fiery as it does from Earth, nineteen times closer. We are a long way from home, and we have to go still further.

## NEPTUNE

In the hinterlands of the solar family, the eighth planet Neptune appears (pic. 56) as an aqua-blue shadow, befitting its namesake, the Roman god of sea. Neptune is the last of the gas giants, and the largest of its thirteen known moons, Triton (pic. 57), has the distinction of being the coldest place in the observed solar system at minus 235 degrees C or minus 391 degrees F . It is also the only major satellite in

29. Andromeda, our nearest large spiral galaxy, is about 2.5 times larger than the Milky Way. These two galaxies are on a course of collision that is estimated to happen 3.5 billion years from now.

30. Example of an elliptic galaxy, where we find no discernible pattern of the rotation of the stars. This is in sharp contrast with the regular rotational pattern of stars in a spiral galaxy.

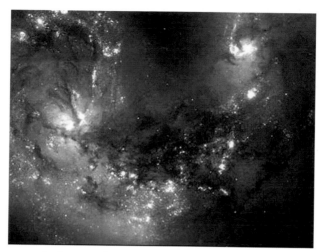

31. Photograph showing the cosmic collision of two spiral galaxies. Some irregular galaxies are formed this way which produce many new stars from the emergent gas and dust clouds.

32. Astronaut Dr Edgar Mitchell on the surface of the moon, who has seen with his own eyes that the moon is just another piece of solid real estate like our Earth. In the near future, a permanent scientific colony on the moon will help us on our journey to other planets.

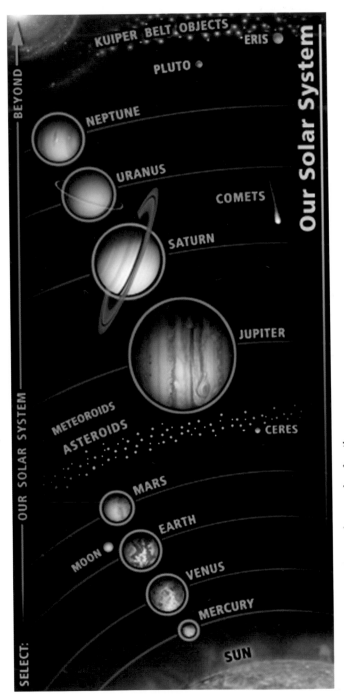

33. The principal members of our solar family.

34. The surface of Mercury, the nearest planet to the Sun.

35. Venus, the second planet from the Sun, is shrouded by a veil of rapidly circulating gas composed of carbon dioxide and sulphur. There is no rain on Venus, but you can observe lightning and thunder almost all the time in its atmosphere.

36. Under its cloud cover, the surface of Venus is solid like Earth, but most of it is covered with volcanic lava. The temperature on its surface is 480 degrees C and the atmospheric pressure is ninety times higher than that on Earth. We need to resolve the mystery why the twin planets, Earth and Venus, have such different atmospheres.

37. An unforgettable picture of Earth rising on the moon.

38. Just like Earth, Mars has ice caps on its poles. In addition, some bluish ice clouds are visible away from the polar caps. We can also see the large dust storms on the surface of Mars.

39. In this historic picture, we see our own Sun setting on Mars.

40. The red clay on the surface of Mars. The colour comes from iron oxide.

41. A dry ravine-like feature and pebbles on the surface of Mars. Surprisingly, there was even flood on Mars at one time.

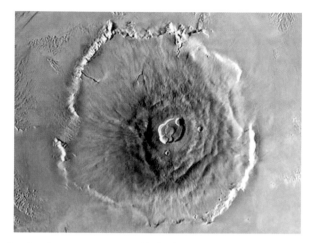

42. The dead volcano on Mars called Olympus Mons. Its peak, 16 miles in height, is three times higher than Mount Everest. There is no other peak higher than this in the solar family.

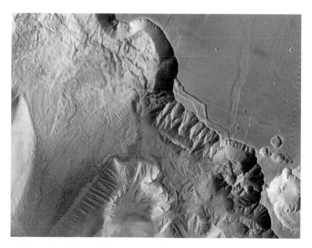

43. Larger than the Grand Canyon is this canyon on Mars, which is four miles deep and 2,500 miles long; a canyon larger than this is not visible anywhere else in our solar system. The ridges indicate past water flow.

44. A large asteroid similar to the one that hit the surface of Earth and possibly caused the dinosaurs to disappear. This asteroid even has a small moon shown on its right.

45. The wounds from parts of a comet hitting the surface of Jupiter look like spots of blood. Also visible is the violent storm in its atmosphere.

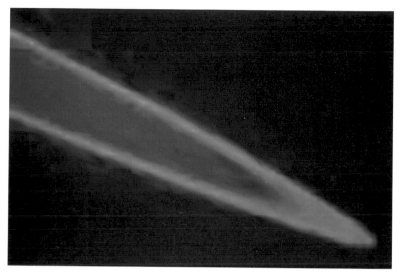

46. Three fine rings of Jupiter.

47. The four moons of Jupiter—Io, Europa, Ganymede, and Callisto. Observing their motions, Galileo first proved that everything is not rotating around Earth.

48. The volcanoes on the surface of Io are still active. Except for Earth and Io, there is no convincing proof of volcanoes existing anywhere in the solar system. The yellow and orange lava is due to the presence of liquid sulphur on the surface of Io.

49. Jupiter's moon, Europa, is covered with ice. The possibility of the existence of life there is being investigated.

50. A montage of Saturn with six of its moons.

51. There are numerous rings around Saturn. They are being shown in different colours to show some details.

52. The largest moon of Saturn is Titan. Its dense atmosphere is shrouding the solid surface below. There is some methane gas in its atmosphere. Man could fly with wings in Titan's atmosphere.

53. Saturn's moon, Dione, looks very much like our moon.

54. A montage of blue-green Uranus with five of its moons.

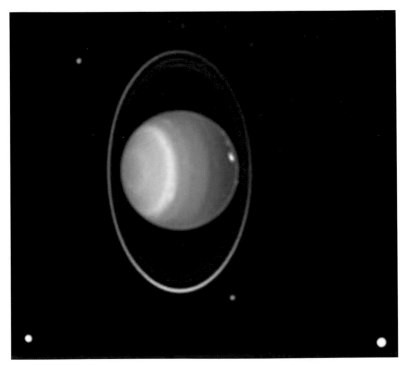

55. Uranus with some of its rings and moons. A reddish cloud is visible in its atmosphere.

the solar system that orbits in a direction opposite to its planet. Quite possibly, Neptune's gravity captured a wandering comet to make Triton its largest satellite.

Neptune's distance from the Sun is a chilly 2.794 billion miles or 4.497 billion kilometres, earning its reputation as an inhabitant of solar Siberia. In this remote and 'timeless' outpost, one year is equal to 165 Earth years.

The atmosphere of Neptune is composed of hydrogen, helium and methane, brewing a dramatic climate with storms of nine times the speed of any on Earth. In fact, no place in the solar system is as stormy as Neptune. To paraphrase the great movie comedian W.C. Fields, planet Neptune is 'a place fit for neither man nor beast'.

The existence of Neptune was predicted in 1843 and it was discovered as the eighth planet in 1846. Like all its gas-giant neighbours in space, it spins fast on its axis, making one rotation in less than an Earth day. Neptune is also encircled by rings. So far, we have observed six.

Apart from the Sun and its four gas giants—Jupiter, Saturn, Uranus and Neptune—all the foremost members of the solar family are solid chunks of real estates (pics. 2, 32), like Earth. If you want to buy land on the cheap some day, there may be plenty of prospects in our solar family. Do you want to buy some land on the moon now? Some enterprising people can already accommodate you.

## PLUTO

Until the year 2006, tiny Pluto—forty times further from the Sun than Earth—was accorded full status as the ninth and outermost planet in the solar family, but it has recently been demoted to the rank of a 'dwarf planet', and it may not be the only one. Scientists have discovered other rocky, icy, round bodies in the neighbourhood with names like Eris and Sedna. Eris is actually larger than Pluto. It is a fact that as our instruments are able to penetrate the secrets of this dark region, more such dwarf planets are being identified. Nonetheless, Pluto remains a member in good standing of the solar family, even though it is named after the god of the underworld.

Pluto has three moons, the closest of which is Charon. Because Charon is nearly half the size of its parent planet, it's a bit of a stretch to call it a moon, and some astronomers refer to Pluto and Charon as a 'double world'. Whatever we choose to call them, they are so far away that it is difficult to know much about them. Very little sunlight reaches Pluto, and much has remained in darkness about it. Recently, however, we have received indirect evidence that an atmosphere exists on Pluto, and that the small planet may be a frozen snowball of gas and dust. NASA has sent a space probe to investigate its hunch that clues to the formation of the solar family 4.5 billion years ago could be hidden inside Pluto and Charon.

## Kuiper Belt to Oort Cloud

We have now returned close to that place where this chapter began, the Kuiper Belt (pic. 58), over a billion miles beyond the orbit of our last planet. If we watch for a while, we are likely to see huge flying icebergs—some as big as small countries—come spinning past us. Members of this forbidding world of ice and rock are called Kuiper Belt Objects, or KBOs. Many are destined to become comets, and may one day wander within Earth's view.

The Kuiper Belt is named for Dutch-American astronomer Gerard Kuiper, who predicted its existence back in the 1950s. As has been said, it is known to scientists mainly as a spawning ground for comets. KBOs are basically big snowballs in space or, more accurately, ice balls spiked with rock. From time to time, one of these snowballs is nudged by gravity from its place in what is known as the scattered disc of the Kuiper Belt and makes a beeline for a new orbit around the Sun. As it approaches the Sun, the ice is vaporized and forms the long tail of a comet. By examining comet dust, we have learned that these icy travellers are 4.5 billion years old. What else is approximately that age? If your answer is the Sun, then your powers of observation are sharpening. The original elements from which the solar family was born are preserved inside comets, which make them some of our oldest solar family relatives. What sort of forensic evidence might we gather from sifting through these primeval snowballs?

We know that comets usually making the circuit in 200 years or less originate in the Kuiper Belt. But other comets, hailing from even more distant outposts, have orbits which take them on a journey lasting thousands and thousands of years. Those comets come from the mysterious Oort Cloud.

In 1950, the Dutch astronomer Jan Oort examined the trajectories of these so-called long period comets and conjectured that their origins must lie well beyond the Kuiper Belt, in a dark region at the very edges of the solar system. This region is now known as the Oort Cloud, and if you want to investigate how our place in space came to be, book your ticket. Going back there is like returning to the place of your birth, and if we can stand the cold, we'll return with our evidence bags full. Cold is an understatement.

Out here, we are 50,000 times further from the Sun than we are on our own planet Earth, and we see it as a distant star. Nonetheless, the Sun's gravitational pull keeps the Oort Cloud as a part of the solar system even at a distance of 7 trillion kilometres.

## SUN

From the furthest reaches of the solar system, let's set our engines for warp speed and blast back towards the centre to pay one last visit to our head of the solar household. On the way, we will make a stop at our base planet, Earth, where we shall set up our observation post, a safe 93,000,000 miles away from the Sun.

The Sun is a giant fireball, as restless as an ocean. Enormous explosions are always occurring on its surface, hurling its fire many thousand miles into the sky. And like an ocean wave, the ejected fire falls back into the Sun. The fusion reaction which lit the Sun nearly 5 billion years ago is still producing the energy to make it shine. All the planets and moons are made observable by reflected sunlight.

But in another 5 billion years, the Sun will have burned through all its hydrogen and will start to become a red giant. During this expansion, the Sun will engulf Mercury and Venus. And what about Earth? The dying red giant will simply melt it. Eventually, the Sun will die and start to cool off. A white dwarf, surrounded by a planetary nebula, will be left. And at the very end, a black dwarf is all that will remain of our once brilliant Sun.

The head of the solar family is now in middle age. What is the secret of the Sun's longevity? We already know. It doesn't run on ordinary fuel. It burns nuclear fuel. To maintain its fire, the Sun burns 600 million tons of hydrogen per second, and still has enough in its store to keep the fires going for another 5 billion years. Before that fuel is exhausted, our descendants will have to find a new address in the universe.

Wherever we do happen to end up, it will have to be in another solar family. We cannot survive without a star. Our food chain is initiated by sunlight through photosynthesis. Our civilization depends upon the fossil fuel created from the energy of the Sun, and very possibly some day soon be able to convert sunlight directly into electricity to solve the energy crisis. The Sun's heat maintains our moderate atmospheric temperature and retains water as a liquid, both essential for the existence of life. Each morning when the Sun rises, remind yourself that you owe your life to it. It may make getting up for school a little easier!

Let us now ponder over any clue we may have gathered by studying our immediate neighbourhood in detail. We see that the conditions can be different at different parts of the solar system. But we do have a habitable zone around our Sun. In the innumerable other solar systems in the universe could there be habitable zones as well? Finding that is another task for the cosmic detectives.

Our Earth, the third planet from the Sun, revolves at distances especially suitable for the evolution of life. It is neither too hot nor too cold; again the temperature is right for water to be in liquid form. Liquid water made it possible for life to appear on Earth after a long 10 billion years of universe making. It wasn't life like it exists today, but it was a start.

After billions of years of complicated evolution and development, human beings with large, curious brains began to populate Earth, and almost immediately started asking questions about where they and their universe had come from. It often seems as if we were made to solve the mysteries of the universe.

We humans are the only ones on this earth who have not ceased to be amazed about the mysteries of the universe. Our questions are endless. Our desire to know is untiring. Our appetite for discovery, analysis and experience is insatiable. We do not know the last word about the universe. And our investigation about it is also endless. However, one thing appears certain. There is some deep connection between man and the universe. I felt it when I was a boy, and I feel it today. I wonder if you are beginning to feel it too.

# The Fingerprints of Creation

We have now completed a field study of our neighbourhood in the cosmos, going planet by planet and covering the ground in search of material evidence that can be found 'close to home'. Together, we have travelled a distance of many light years. We have also ventured into the great expanse of deep space, asking questions about the universe and receiving some answers. Now it is time to review our files and begin to assemble our case, and the questions—as in any detective's investigation—are *Who? What? When? Where?* . . . and *Why?* To these essential queries, we might add a big *How?*

*Who* is responsible for all of this? *What* is the true nature of the universe at its deepest level? *When* did it begin, if indeed it had a beginning? *Where* did it start from and where is it going? *Why* was it created? This last question goes to the most important issue of 'motive' in any investigation by a detective. Could our own eventual emergence have had something to do with that motive? And finally: *how* did such an enormous abundance of energy come out of nowhere? Do we have evidence that will allow us to solve the mystery? Actually, we have more than you probably realize.

Let's return for a moment to the story of Edwin Hubble, sitting inside the great dome of Mt Wilson Observatory in

California with his eyes glued to the telescope. Do you remember his most important discovery? He found that the galaxies were racing away from one another in all directions from some central starting gate, and that the further away they were, the faster they were moving. Hubble did not venture to say what point of origin they were receding from, nor did he explain how that point could seem to be everywhere! He simply fixed his gaze on the far out nebulae, using the largest telescope of his day, and reported the evidence as he saw it.

Let me remind you of something else. Like most people of his time, the great physicist Albert Einstein believed that the universe was unchanging—neither increasing nor decreasing in size—even though his own equations indicated that the universe could not be static! Like many world-class detectives before him, he couldn't quite believe the implications of his own investigation. A piece of forensic evidence was needed, and Edwin Hubble provided it with the red shift of the Cepheid variable stars in the Andromeda galaxy. The universe was not static at all. Hubble gave convincing proof that the universe was dramatically expanding. But expanding from what?

It took another twenty years of detective work to make any progress based on Hubble's discovery. Among the scientists who did the 'legwork' were Georges Lemaitre and George Gamow. They put the issue on the table: if the future was taking the galaxies further and further apart, would it not then stand to reason that in the past they must have been closer together? They adopted an analogy from the movies, which were just becoming a popular new form of entertainment, and asked what would happen if we ran the movie of the universe in reverse, from present to past. By 'running the frames backwards' using Einstein's equations, they showed that the galaxies were indeed coming closer and closer, converging on some incredibly ancient and incredibly compacted beginning.

Ultimately—in somewhat the same manner as a collapsing star triggering a supernova becomes a black hole—all the matter in the universe would be squeezed into such a tight space that its compression due to the effects of gravity might result in what Einstein's equations called a *singularity*, a point where the laws of physics would simply break down. But before coming to this point, all the matter in the universe would be converted by the tremendous heat into almost pure energy. Remember: heat is generated when matter is compressed. Can you imagine how high the temperature would be if the whole universe was compressed into the size of an orange?

This fact of physics pointed to clues that finally made the case for a cosmic explosion as the 'birth cry' of our universe, and the event that launched its expansion. At first, this idea sounded crazy to many scientists. The British astronomer Fred Hoyle, who didn't buy it, coined the term 'Big Bang' to describe such an explosion. He was trying to make a joke, but it turned out to be no joke at all.

'Bang?' you ask. 'As in a very big noise?'

Well, no. A noise—big or little—requires a medium like air to carry the sound waves. There was no such medium before the existence of space. It is important to recall what we touched on earlier: that the Big Bang was an explosion of space itself and not an explosion in any pre-existing space. In the universe today, it is the space between galaxies that is expanding. If you can picture this, space is being stretched. Will it stretch forever?

Now, as detectives, we need what the police call a 'smoking gun'. We can't simply pin the birth of the universe on the Big Bang without some fingerprints. What proof do we have that it really happened? George Gamow theorized in the 1940s that an explosion stupendous enough to bring a universe into being would leave a kind of 'afterglow' throughout space. (Try to remember the last time you saw a fireworks show. The really big ones leave a luminous imprint in the sky.) Gamow—a true cosmic detective—calculated that although the expansion of the universe over billions of years would cool the primordial ball of fire, traces of its initial heat would still be found today, scattered evenly throughout the cosmos in the form of microwaves. If so, these traces would be part of the fingerprints of creation.

In 1965, Arno Penzias and Robert Wilson, two young radio astronomers at Bell Labs, New Jersey, accidentally found Gamow's predicted microwave relic of the Big Bang using a big horn antenna that picked up radio waves from all across the sky. It is true that detectives sometimes find the most important clues in places they don't even expect to find them! They kept hearing a hissing sound coming over the speakers, but had no idea at first that what they were hearing was the energy of creation itself, and that this energy was everywhere. Literally everywhere! Talk about evidence. This was the clincher.

You can observe the evidence for yourself right now. Be prepared: it's a little spooky once you think about it. If you are near a television, turn it on and switch to a channel with nothing on. Now, take a moment to contemplate the static you see on your screen and the hissing noise that accompanies it. Let your eyes go a little lazy until the dots begin to dance. You are looking in part at a very ancient fingerprint, because a percentage of that static is the microwave remnant of the fiery birth of the universe. This remnant is called Cosmic Microwave Background Radiation, or CMBR.

The discovery of this cosmic background radiation marks the beginning of cosmology as a reputable scientific discipline. Cosmology left the realm of myth and entered the court of hard evidence.

Good detectives are sceptical by nature, and CMBR takes a little getting used to. You don't have to take anything on faith. There is more dramatic evidence yet. The Big Bang theory is what scientists call a model, and good models can be tested and verified. If there was a Big Bang, it came with such astounding heat that only the very heartiest forms of matter could possibly have arisen during its first few seconds and fractions of seconds. In the beginning, this would have meant the existence of mostly energy with just the slightest dusting of proto-matter. The fundamental particles we now recognize as the basic constituents of matter would have gradually congealed from this 'soup' as the universe cooled through expansion.

But by one second after the Big Bang, the temperature had fallen to 10 billion degrees, and the universe was like a giant thermonuclear reactor gradually cooling down by expansion. Our knowledge of the rate of nuclear processes, clocked and tested in decades of laboratory experiments, allows us to predict the ratio of atomic elements that would be produced in such a reactor.

The first three to four minutes should have produced 75 per cent hydrogen and 25 per cent helium, with a tiny bit of other light elements like lithium, and this is indeed what we find at the scene of our investigation. In order for our evidence to hold up in court, we must have a perfect match.

If hydrogen and helium are counted together as one billion, then the proportion of lithium should be about one. And this is exactly what we observe. Therefore, our evidence is accurate to nearly one part per billion, and that is exceedingly accurate! Excellent accuracy is also observed for deuterium. This third proof should give you much more confidence in presenting your case.

The first three to four minutes of creation were critical, as this was when the light elements—mainly hydrogen and helium—were produced. The heavier atomic elements up to iron, as we have learned, were subsequently forged in stellar furnaces. The rest of the elements were literally made in the shockwaves of exploding stars, the supernovae.

Now it's time to separate the hobbyists from the pros, for our investigation requires answers to some more basic questions. What was it that 'banged'? How did it become a universe? How did the universe come to be so smooth on the large scale, as indicated by the high degree of uniformity of the microwave background radiation, and yet be so lumpy, that is, clumped into stars, galaxies, and clusters of galaxies, on the 'local' scale? How has the universe reached such an advanced age, indicated to be more than 13 billion years? Why did it not collapse in on itself by the force of gravity or fly apart from the thrust of expansion? The rate of this expansion had to be very finely tuned to have allowed the universe to survive to the present day. And most puzzling of all, what produced the enormous energy of the Big Bang fireball itself?

You can pick up some clues from another cosmic detective, scientist Alan Guth. In 1979, Alan Guth proposed the inflationary theory of universal expansion. Not the sort of inflation you see when the price of milk suddenly rises at the store, but a colossal physical inflation of space that occurred in the very early universe, an expansion unimaginably faster than the observed expansion of the universe today. It might sound like science fiction to you, but Einstein's equations indicate that under certain very special circumstances, gravity can be a *repulsive* rather than an attractive force. Were these circumstances present at the very beginning? Alan Guth found some indication of it. And if so, the universe would have gone from zero to hero in much less time than it takes you to sneeze.

Guth glimpsed the possibility of a repulsive gravity in the first blink of the newly awakened universe. He showed that this repulsive force could almost instantaneously expand the infant universe from a nugget of space much smaller than an atom to the size of an orange. Don't underestimate how big an increase this is. It is on the order of 1 with at least 30 zeroes after it. This is why it is called inflation.

Do we really have any proof that such inflation indeed happened? Yes, we now have some convincing evidences, as we shall see shortly. But first we may have to adjust our model slightly to allow for a two-stage genesis—a Big Whimper before the Big Bang. As in an innocuously lit fuse causing a huge explosion! Again, for simplicity in visualizing this, let us consider a two-dimensional model.

Have you ever watched an artisan blow molten glass into the shape of a vase or a sphere? When he first begins to force air into the blowing tube, the hot glass remains for a moment 'stuck' as a tiny bubble, as if it were resisting the artisan's effort to shape it into something else, something greater. Then, very suddenly, it begins to expand, rapidly becoming a sphere. The same sort of thing happens when you chew bubblegum and try to blow a bubble. At first, nothing happens but a little blister, no matter how hard you blow. It's stuck. And then it's not.

The inflation theory of cosmic origins suggests that the infant universe also got 'stuck' for a moment at the threshold of birth, like a baby not quite ready to leave the safe harbour of its mother's womb. And then, in an instant, it was out and hasn't stopped growing since!

When molten glass is blown into a beautiful bauble, whatever slight imperfections or marks of identity are in the material will still be there when it is blown up—only stretched and smoothed out. The same is true of the universe.

Do you know why the universe is so smooth on the large scale? You will find the clue in inflation. Recall that before inflation the universe occupied a very tiny nugget of space. Within this infinitesimal space, it was possible for the content of the universe to be in a state of thermal balance and the raw material was more or less evenly distributed, like a nearly perfect glob of molten glass. This thermal balance remained intact when the universe suddenly expanded, giving it smoothness on the large scale.

However, keep in mind that I said 'like a *nearly* perfect glob of molten glass'. There were a few distinguishing marks in the stuff of the natal cosmos, and as amazing as it seems, they are still visible today—but stretched out—in the cosmic background radiation.

We now have some understanding about how the universe started close to its beginning and commenced to expand, and also of the force which drove its expansion. But what about the force of gravity, the force that makes a ball fall back to earth when it is thrown into the air? Why does gravity not make the universe stop expanding and fall back in on itself, as happens with collapsing stars that produce black holes?

The clue again can be found in inflation, which set the rate of cosmic expansion to a precision of better than 1 part in 10 to the fiftieth power, or 1 followed by fifty zeroes. And the reason that the balance between expansion and contraction (repulsion and attraction) is still maintained is that there happens to be exactly the right amount of 'stuff' in the universe. One speck more or less and the universe would have either collapsed in a 'Big Crunch' or ended in a runaway expansion.

That 'stuff' (matter and all forms of energy) now includes you and me. So it is, in fact, scientifically accurate to say that the universe would not be complete without you. Each one of us is an essential ingredient for the soundness of the universe.

As for the question where the cosmic fireball itself came from, the clue is also provided by inflation that tells us something remarkable about energy. The process of inflation created all the positive energy in the universe, but at the same time it also created an equal amount of negative energy in the form of the mutual gravitational attraction of the stuff of the universe.

Mathematical analyses show that, to this very day, the sum total of positive energy in the universe equals the sum total of negative energy. The cosmos today may be bigger and lumpier, but it contains exactly the energy it started out with. You know that when you put identical quantities on both sides of an equation, they cancel each other out. Therefore, again strange as it may sound, the total energy of the universe was, is, and always will be zero.

But wait a second; how can something as big, bright, and busy as the universe have zero energy? A hint: it can, if the energy of inflation arose from something with the value of zero. This was pointed out by Alan Guth in his famous remark, 'It is said that there's no such thing as a free lunch, but the universe is the ultimate free lunch.'

Now our detective inspection is reaching its final stage, because we are about to witness the birth pang of the universe. For that, we depend primarily on experimental results from the field of high energy particle physics. This is the study of the very, very small subatomic particles as opposed to the observation of the very, very large stars and galaxies practised in astronomy.

As we retrace our steps back towards its origin, the universe becomes much smaller and the temperature increasingly higher. Such temperatures are available only in particle accelerators, which are a kind of big microscope for physicists to view the unseen world of subatomic space. Temperatures created in particle accelerators can replicate the condition of the early universe up to a trillion degrees that existed after about a microsecond of the Big Bang. So, as cosmic detectives you can have some confidence in determining what the early universe looked like up to that time.

The particle physicists also look to the relics of the events of the early universe to provide support for their theories, because at temperatures higher than what is attainable by super particle colliders, the only resource available for particle physicists is the study of the early universe itself. This symbiotic relationship of particle physics (which deals with the smallest) and cosmology (the study of the largest) has provided essential forensic links in our detective investigation of the cosmic origin.

Also, thanks to COBE satellite, the Hubble Space Telescope, and a host of other 'eyes' in the sky, as well as the availability of high speed computers, we can probe the

56. Neptune, where violent storms exist in the atmosphere that are nine times faster than on Earth. No other planet has faster storm than this. The blue colour of Neptune is due to absorption by methane, just like that on Uranus.

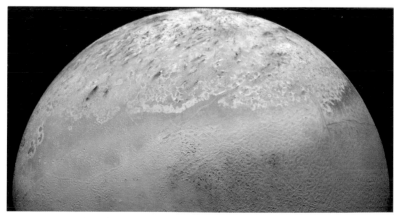

57. Triton is the largest moon among the thirteen moons of Neptune. No colder place than Triton exists in the observable solar family.

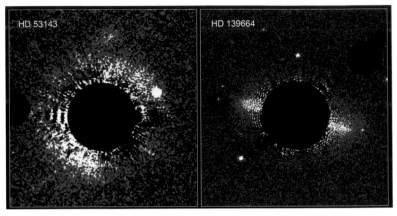

58. After the eight planets of the solar system is the Kuiper Belt, which could look like this. The dwarf planets Pluto and Eris were created in this belt. Comets coming from this belt reappear within 200 years or less.

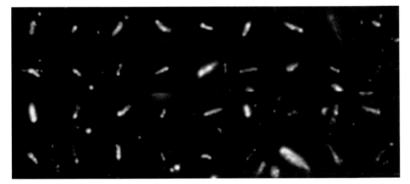

59. One billion years after the Big Bang, the galaxies look like this. The width of this picture is about the size of our Milky Way. The galaxies of today were formed by the aggregation of these primordial galaxies. Such a picture demonstrates how the baby universe matured to its adulthood.

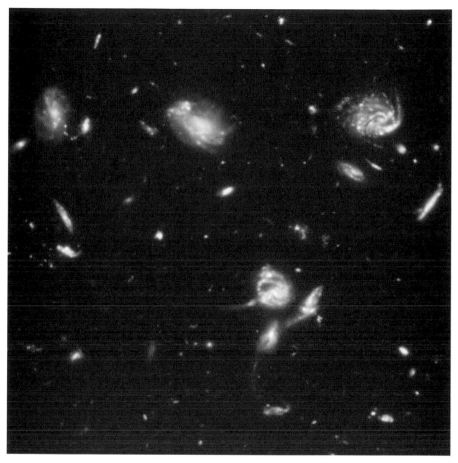

60. Another example of primordial galaxies combining to form large mature galaxies.

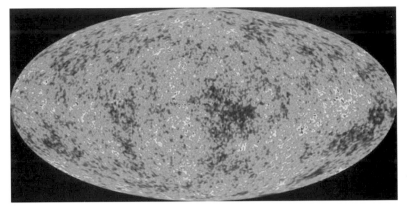

61. The stretch marks of the birth of the universe taken by the WMAP satellite, the successor to COBE. An analysis of these marks gives us a glimpse of the moment close to the birth of the universe.

62. The timeline of the biography of the universe prepared with the help of data taken by the WMAP satellite, indicating that everything in this universe could come from a single source.

cosmos as never before, using the entire spectrum of electromagnetic radiation from radio waves to gamma rays. This allows us to examine the universe in unprecedented details and to continue uncovering cosmic relics like those that have ushered the golden age of cosmology.

The Hubble Space Telescope has presented us with the first ever evidence of a black hole, which should support our premise that the mass energy of tens of billions of galaxies indeed could have been packed into an insignificant niche, just as is thought to have been the case in the early universe.

As we have learned, when we gaze far out into space with the benefit of wondrous tools like the Hubble telescope, we are looking back in time, because it takes billions of years for the light to reach us from a galaxy far away. Through the looking glass of Hubble, the early galaxies (pics. 59, 60), which evolved a few billion years after the Big Bang, look less elegantly symmetrical than the more regular galaxies we observe closer at hand, thus providing another clue to the growth of the baby universe into its adulthood. You can count this as an additional evidence of the evolution of our universe from the Big Bang. But in order to witness the moment of cosmic birth, we have to go further.

What happens when we 'reverse the frames' further, to a place with even higher temperatures and greater density? The most breathtaking answer comes by way of the COBE satellite. With its ear trained on the murmur of the cosmic background radiation, COBE has detected minute variations in the primordial fabric of spacetime: stretch marks (pic. 61) from the cosmic dawn. These scars appear like hieroglyphic squiggles, smeared across space by its inflationary expansion. Stephen Hawking called these findings 'the scientific discovery of the century, if not all time'. *Newsweek* magazine dubbed them 'the handwritings of God'. The Nobel Prize in physics in 2006 was awarded for this discovery. Why such excitement?

Well, to put it plainly, the excitement is because what we are seeing is part of the blueprint for our universe, enfolded in spacetime close to its beginning. Scientists have long had difficulty in determining how the galaxies arose from something as smooth and homogenous as the pure energy of the Big Bang. It is as if you were stirring a creamy sauce on the stovetop and suddenly noticed little lumps—more and more with each passing second—beginning to form in the sauce. Where did they come from? Were the seeds of these lumps in the sauce all along?

According to quantum theory, there were some wrinkles in primordial spacetime. As space expanded abruptly due to inflation, these wrinkles were stretched out, but not eliminated. They are detectable to us today as exceedingly small variations in the temperature of the microwave background radiation, and they are the seeds of galaxies.

From our field investigation of the existing galaxies in the universe, we found an indication of the kinds of seeds that would have been required to produce these galaxies. The characteristics of these seeds agree very well with those observed by COBE and predicted by the inflationary theory. The coincidence of the predicted and observed characteristics gives us substantial confidence that inflation did happen and its theory can get us close to the moment of delivery. There are also some other evidences in support of inflation, making the theory more or less established in most scientists' minds.

The squiggles in the microwave background radiation observed by the COBE satellite are a cosmic decoder. They have, among other things, allowed us to fix the age of the universe at 13.7 billion years with an extraordinary accuracy of 1 per cent. Combined with other measurements, COBE data also confirmed what the universe is made of today: 4 per cent ordinary matter, 23 per cent dark matter of an as yet unknown composition, and about 73 per cent of a mysterious factor known as dark energy. There are a number of ideas about what dark matter may be, but dark energy is a phantom. What we do know is that dark energy has an effect of repulsive gravity similar to that which drove the cosmic inflation, and may be a significant factor in the continuing development of the universe.

With the help of the theory of inflation, our cosmic detective story can account for everything in the nearly 14-billion-year history of the universe, but for a tiny fraction of a second after its moment of creation. The trail of evidence has led the detectives who came before you to the edge of a cosmological abyss. The sudden rush of cosmic inflation has erased all the evidence. Does our search end here? Will we ever be able to glimpse past inflation to the moment of inception? Must we stamp the case UNSOLVED? Certainly not. There are more alluring clues to be pursued.

Particle physicists are close to proof that at least everything physical in this universe comes from a single source. Let me explain what I mean by 'single source'. Our universe is highly complex. There are, for instance, a multiplicity of plant and animal species and a multiplicity of chemical elements that form them. We have seen that there is an array of cosmic phenomena: red giants, white dwarfs, neutron stars, gas planets, rocky planets, etc. Everywhere we look, we see an enormous variety. All things we see are so different that it is almost impossible to imagine they could come from a single source. Yet, amazingly, that's what is being indicated by the latest findings of modern cosmology and quantum theory.

Supported by the extrapolation of our laboratory measurements, it seems reasonable to conclude that this one source is what we would discover if we could time travel back to before the Big Bang and inflation. Could such a source indeed exist at the beginning of the universe? We don't know for sure. However, it appears to be consistent with what you see in the timeline diagram (pic. 62) of the universe prepared with the help of the data taken by the MAP satellite, which strongly suggests that everything could come from one single source. But what is it? What source could create a universe?

These questions highlight the final and greatest mystery to be investigated by you and other cosmic detectives. As you cover the ground, looking for clues, you will encounter other members of this club, and other theories about the origin of the cosmos. Some theories will be highly mathematical, some will even sound metaphysical. One thing seems fairly certain: whatever the single source is, it is almost certainly not something you can hold in your hand. We have gone far beyond that. Could it be that the quality we call consciousness is a critical element for the creation of our universe?

There is a tantalizing clue folded into what is known as the *anthropic principle*, an idea perhaps best summed up by the noted physicist Freeman Dyson's statement that 'the universe must have known we were coming'. The anthropic principle argues that the universe evolved as it did, so that we humans could come along to figure it out! At inception the universe was so small that it had to obey the traffic laws of quantum theory. According to these laws, the universe could have been born in innumerable different ways. But how our universe came to be the way it is from all these countless possibilities? Perhaps the most famous scientist of our time, Stephen Hawking, says, 'The anthropic principle can be given a precise formulation, and it seems essential when dealing with the origin of the universe.' In other words, the evolution of conscious beings like us had to be a necessary condition for the beginning of our universe. Put this in your case file and chew over it a bit. Is it possible that our long and painstaking investigation is a circle leading right back to us?

If there is reason to believe that consciousness is an essential ingredient of our universe, then how is it related to the material world today? We can find some clues from our study of modern science. For example, in quantum physics, the wave and particle aspects exist simultaneously and inseparably. Also, Einstein showed that space, time and field are magnificently intertwined in their existence; they cannot exist separately. These examples pave the path for accepting the simultaneous and inseparable existence of two primary realities such as matter and consciousness.

The mystery, however, is still not solved beyond a reasonable doubt. We must continue to investigate, asking from where, how, and why consciousness arose and how exactly it is linked to the physical manifestation. Is consciousness connected to the most important part of our investigation—the motive? This is your assignment. It may take all your life to complete this, and even then, you may still wonder. Most detective stories are wrapped up neatly at the end. There is no guarantee this one will be, but its pursuit could be as much fun as its solution.

# The Story in the Stars

At the conclusion of many classic mysteries, the detective gathers all the principal characters in the parlour and announces the results of his or her investigation. In our detective story, of course, we are not investigating a crime but an act of creation and the mystery is all the deeper. As suggested in the previous chapter, it may not lend itself to a simple wrap-up, and it will probably take many detectives—not just one intrepid gumshoe—to solve it. Even then, can it really be solved completely?

Are there some things in the cosmos that are simply unknowable? Could we ever know precisely *why* the universe came into existence when it did? The *motive* is often the most difficult thing for a detective to establish. Regardless of whether or not we finally deduce the *why* of the universe, we have come within a minute fraction of a second of understanding the *how*, and that may be enough to allow us to consider the case closed for now—or, at any rate, not completely unsolved. Most importantly, though, the inference of our investigation will make us see the world and ourselves in a radically different way.

What message is dispersed throughout the universe for us? What words are scrawled by the stars in the tablet of the night sky? You may come to see that the primary message from the biography of the universe is oneness, for it appears that *we have all come from one single source.* We can trace the roots of our family tree to the beginning of the universe 13.7 billion years ago. At that time, of course, there was no sign of life, but the potentiality of life was in the blueprint of the universe, just as the blueprint of a tree is contained in a seed.

Today, whether we are black, white, brown or yellow or whether we are Hindu, Christian, Muslim, Buddhist or Jewish, we are members of the same family. We are all cosmic kins tied from our birth to the sun, the stars, the planets, the moons, and the whole universe itself. There is no essential difference between us. If we remember that we share the same origin, all lines of division will be erased. This message of oneness has been forged in the fireball of the universe. It should give us great inspiration to go forward forgetting all our differences.

I began this book by recalling that once upon a time I had believed there was a story written in the stars. A story in which, somehow, even a poor, isolated boy like myself played the role of a prince. I did not know then that Albert Einstein, the greatest scientist of the last century, had already said that each one of us is at the centre of the universe. This may puzzle you if you're used to thinking of the universe as something like a big globe or a bubble growing larger and larger. A sphere has a centre, right? Well, the universe is a special kind of a sphere whose centre happens to be everywhere. So whether you live in a sparkling city like New York or Paris, or a small, dusty town on the edge of nowhere, you can truly say that you live at the centre of the cosmos.

A related message comes loud and clear through the chapters of the cosmic biography. It is a message of empowerment: *none of us is insignificant.* We may be small, and our power limited, but if we have understood the story in the stars, we know that the universe is not complete without us. This is neither fable nor romantic fantasy, but scientific fact. We know also that we are not only an inseparable and necessary part of the physical universe, but that the very blueprint of the cosmos provided for our eventual emergence.

Are you wondering why we are so essential? Here we face probably the strangest and most wondrous fact of all, one we touched upon in the previous section. The eminent physicist John Wheeler said it most eloquently, 'It is incontrovertible that the observer is a participant in genesis.' Let's contemplate that statement to be sure we understand how astounding it is. Genesis is the beginning of time, the birth of the cosmos. The 'observer' consists of our conscious awareness, the faculty we employ when we look deep and far back into space and time. Are you beginning to get the picture?

Einstein said, 'The most incomprehensible fact about nature is that it is comprehensible.' What he wished to convey is that the universe, for all its mystery, runs on some distinct fundamental laws. Through science, our consciousness is able to observe these laws in action throughout the cosmos. Nobel physicist Eugene Wigner chimed in by stating that there are two miracles: one is the existence of the unfailing laws of nature, and the other is the ability of the human mind to divine them. The distinguished British mathematician Sir Roger Penrose is also bemused by the fact that the universe has developed in obedience of laws that our consciousness seems designed to grasp. Could it be that our consciousness is indeed inherently linked to the universal blueprint? So it is a circle, or a loop, which keeps coming back to you and me, emphasizing our significance time and again.

As we look out at the sky full of stars, I hope we can say: transform us with your fire. Forge us into fully conscious beings. We should listen for the song of oneness among the innumerable stars and hope their song will unite with our own to finally banish the ignorance that causes prejudice and war in our fractious world today.

We know there is great suffering in the world, as well as the everyday disappointment and ugliness. But you can rise above all of this if you recognize yourself as an indispensable part of this entire universe, and try to comprehend your kinship with the stars. Remember that we are all made of stardust. That bond of affinity can never be destroyed.

A final word: if we do indeed come from the same source that brought the universe into being, how do we describe this source? What is it made of? Where did it come from? Investigating these questions is your ultimate assignment, and I expect it will keep you on the trail for some time. It is hard work, but I can assure you that once you take this case, you will never give up.

# Index

# Copyright Acknowledgements

## Image Credits

| Image no. | Credits |
| --- | --- |
| 1. | NASA/JPL |
| 2. | NASA/JPL |
| 3. | NASA/COBE Science Team |
| 4. | NASA/JPL |
| 5. | The Hubble Heritage Team (AURA/STScI/NASA) |
| 6. | NASA/ESA and The Hubble Heritage (STScI, AURA)-ESA/Hubble Collaboration |
| 7. | NASA |
| 8. | NASA, ESA and The Hubble Heritage Team (STScI/AURA) |
| 9. | The COBE Project, DIRBE, NASA |
| 10. | NASA, A.Caulet St-ECF, ESA |
| 11. | NASA, ESA, M. Robberto (STScI/ESA) and the HST Orion Treasury Project Team |
| 12. | NASA Headquarters—Greatest Images of NASA (NASA-HQ-GRIN) |
| 13. | NASA, ESA and J. Hester (ASU) |
| 14. | Mark McCaughrean (Max-Planck-Institute for Astronomy, C. Robert O'Dell (Rice University), and NASA |
| 15. | Created by Tatiana Chekhova, Cosmotoons, Inc. from NASA website images |
| 16. | Judithhh (UTC), released to public domain through Wikimedia Commons |
| 17. | NASA |
| 18. | NASA and The Hubble Heritage Team (STScI/AURA) |
| 19. | NASA, A. Fruchter, ERO Team, STScI |

20. The Hubble Heritage Team (NASA/AURA/STScI)
21. NASA/ESA, R. Sankrit and W. Blair (Johns Hopkins University)
22. NASA
23. NASA, ESA and The Hubble Heritage Team (STScI/AURA)
24. NASA, ESA, J. Hester and A. Loll (Arizona State University)
25. NASA/CXC/ASU/HST/J. Hester et al.
26. NASA and Jeffrey Kenney and Elizabeth Yale (Yale University)
27. NASA/ESA/STScI-PRC1990-20
28. Kirk Borne (STScI) and NASA
29. John Lanoue, released to public domain through Wikimedia Commons
30. NASA, ESA and The Hubble Heritage (STScI/AURA)-ESA/Hubble Collaboration
31. Brad Whitmore (STScI) and NASA
32. Astronaut Dr Edgar Mitchell
33. NASA/JPL
34. NASA/John Hopkins University APL/Carnegie Institution of Washington
35. NASA
36. NASA/JPL
37. NASA
38. NASA, ESA and The Hubble Heritage Team (STScI/AURA)
39. NASA/JPL
40. NASA/JPL
41. NASA/JPL-Caltech/Cornell
42. NASA
43. NASA/JPL
44. NASA/JPL
45. NASA and HST Comet Team
46. NASA/Johns Hopkins University APL/Southwest Research Institute
47. NASA/K. Noll (STScI), J. Spencer (Lowell Ovservatory)
48. NASA/JPL
49. NASA/JPL
50. NASA/JPL
51. NASA
52. NASA/JPL
53. NASA/JPL
54. NASA/JPL
55. NASA
56. NASA/JPL
57. NASA/JPL
58. NASA, ESA, and P. Kalas (UC Berkeley)
59. NASA, A. Straughn, S. Cohen, and R. Windhorst (Arizona State University), and the HUDF team (STScI)
60. NASA, ESA, S. Beckwith (STScI) and the HUDF Team
61. NASA/WMAP Science Team
62. NASA/WMAP Science Team